HORSES SEE US AS WE ARE

NAHSHON COOK

Copyright © 2022 by Nahshon Cook
Cover Artwork by Forrest Morgan

ALL RIGHTS RESERVED. No part of this book may be reproduced or transmitted in any form by any means, electronic or mechanical, including photocopying and recording, or by any information storage and retrieval system, except as may be expressly permitted in writing from the publisher.

Requests for permission should be addressed to:
Nova's Books LLC
PO Box 1685
Parker, CO 80134

ISBN 978-1-7374655-1-5

Introduction

Hello again!

For those of you who don't know me, my name is Nahshon. I would like you to welcome you to my latest collection of stories with a story:

Yesterday, I had a lesson with a student, who is also a trainer and teacher. She came in and asked if we could work on the isolation of the hind legs so that she could learn to better feel the horse's movement in her body, then began to try and give me excuses as to why it wasn't possible. I told her that self-deprecation and excuses aren't allowed in my arena.

After a while passed, we began doing work to start introducing the the canter flying changes. Keeping in mind how Oliveira said that the flying changes are just the asking of one canter lead out of the other (or something close to that), we did working counter-canter down the long sides of the school, walked in the corners, and did collected canter on the short side of the school. After a few rounds of that, instead of going from working counter-canter, to walk, to collected canter, we just went from working counter-canter down the wall with a lead change in the corner and into collected canter on the short side. The change was clean, we celebrated, and I ended the lesson.

When my student dismounted and unbridled her horse, she said, "Thanks for not taking my shit." I said, "You're welcome."

This is a book about healthy relationships, how the practice of horse-humanship helps us find them, and how bumpy the road to better can sometimes be when we let go of those dysfunctions that we could otherwise choose to keep by learning to be as intentionally available as possible to ourselves, our horses, and each other.

Horsehumanship is about trust. Trust is not a conscious effort. Trust is a result of consistency. My small herd of healing soul-wounded equids is guiding me along this path of listening without the fear of losing by teaching me that boundaries become love by not seeing continuously refusing to be hurt as a bad thing. Right now, I'm learning how to be strong enough to serve and not feel inferior. No matter where you are, there you are. Following the horse and finding heaven in ever step is as far as I've gotten.

Some of these stories have been previously published in print, or online. For others, this is the first time they've been seen in public. The golden thread stitching each one to the other is my exploration of trying to teach my students, with a classical dressage rooted pedagogy, how to effectively work with and ride their horses in a way where the past doesn't rob them of who they are right now, in this present moment, with their horse.

This way of working with and riding horses that I teach is not built around the need for perfection. But rather, a devotion to the process of becoming. There are camouflaged charters misrepresenting our true selves to try and protect us from the challenges of living life that horses require us to explore in order to find a clear connection that isn't based on control. Sometimes, those places are hidden deep down in parts of ourselves that we've run away from for a very long time. This book is for people who are tired of running.

1]

Ok, so breathing is a big thing. What point of reference does your stuck-ness have in the rest of life to make your body not work when you're on your horse? You don't have to answer that if you don't want to. But, I think it's important for you to see where you go when that happens.

Right, and I think the challenge is allowing yourself to become more aware of the damming up of energy that makes that flow not impossible. When you feel that stuck-point today let me know. When you feel it coming, I don't want you to second guess it. We're not gonna push through. Because when we push through, we can't feel. When you push through, you're in survival mode.

Good. Walk around the school. Drop your stirrups, and we're gonna try and make your middle just a little bit more stable because you have a really long torso. So, what I want you to think about trying to manage this swiveliness in your hip and your SI joint…push your belly out as far as you can. And then, think about pulling your belt buckle up to your belly button. It'll stretch your lower back. Bring your shoulders over your hips, don't lean back so far. Yeah, that's a little bit better. Good, and relax. Did you just feel how he changed?

Now, there's a debate that seems like it will go on for as long as people are practicing dressage about whether or not you sit on your two seat bones or your two seat bones and your pubic bone. And, I've heard, and I'm not saying anybody is right, I'm just saying, you know, that in the art of reaching sound conclusions you have to listen to both sides of the argument, so that you can make a decision.

And people have talked about men's and women's pelvises being different, all of that stuff, and, of course it's true. But, I don't know if it really matters or not. I'm not saying that it doesn't, I'm just don't know if it does. I've seen many women ride in a beautiful three-point seat, and do a wonderful job with their horse.

The difference between the two seats is how we engage the muscles, right? If you're sitting on just your two seat bones, what has a tendency to happen is that both move in the same direction at the same time, regardless of which of the horse's hind legs is moving under your body. So every time the horse has his or her hind legs under his or her body, it's like ice cream scooping up and forward, and your middle becomes super strong while your balance becomes hard to maintain because you're engaging the inner abdominal muscles.

And this tends to lock your lower back wide open—in hyperextension, and there's not much movement. And so, you're riding the horse's bones instead of the horse's muscles. And all of it has to do with back lengthening: if you push your belly out, your movement falls in line with the natural curve of the spine and compresses the lumbar vertebrae together. But, if you push your belly out and then lift your belt buckle up to your belly button, you'll feel your outer abdominal muscles engage.

Good. Now, when the outer abdominal muscles engage, it makes it really hard to slouch because you've expanded your rib cage out, which automatically opens your chest. And, I think what's important in your situation, is that when you're ribs are open, and your chest is open, not by being forced open with pulled back shoulders, and tight elbows, but by being allowed to open, your diaphragm and your lungs lower, and you're taking deeper breaths in to your body.

The deeper and fuller the breath... Because, generally, if we're here, with a pulled-in abdomen, we oftentimes don't breathe deep down into our lungs. We breathe deep down and shallowly.

Generally, if we're pulling our stomach in to straighten our back, it closes our hip-flexors and turns our knees out, which pulls the backs of our seat bones closer together, which, with sensitive backed horses, can cause them to invert because of the pressure. And because we don't have a base of support to balance we become like a gymnast trying to not fall off the balance beam. Because you're not supported in the movement of the horse's body, you must balance to stay on. This is why it's important: the more you're able to isolate and articulate your joints, the more subtle your aids. You can make your seat deep without becoming heavier with your belly out, and rotating the toes in toward the horse's elbow from your hip socket and acts as a restraining aid for a half-halt or a downward transition. Turn your toes out a bit and bring your heels in, while you have a driving aid. There's a whole lot of variability. Open your heels now, but spread your pinky toe so that your leg becomes long. Your groin muscle should now be contracted.

Too many people ride like they're afraid of their horses. It's all about staying on. Just getting on and hoping not to fall is not correct riding, you see what I mean? It's not what you say that matters. It's where you say it from. The alignment is what allows you to carry yourself. Your position is your voice. Look at how beautifully your horse has begun to relax. Now he can start bringing his hind legs through his back to your hands. Good work!

2]

Sometimes, working with certain horse-bodied ones is like overhearing a Machiavellian conversation in the other room about how being so shut down that you're always going out of your way to be nice out of your fear of anger; which is better than your sadness, after not having anywhere to go in a long time, then finally exploding, like a bomb out of a volcano. A preparation for harder things and the kind of grace that harder things bring in the form of clear-eyed focus that wipes all emotion away.

There are some things we don't see, not because they're not there, but because we don't understand what's standing right in front of us. I once gave a lesson to a person whose horse they were riding, a really nice sorrel gelding, had killed a man when he was just a three-year-old colt: It was his former trainer, who, apparently, was known for running his horses into the ground. Some might say the guy was just downright brutal. The poor fella died of a hole from a hoof in the center his chest.

When the hard work of trying to help with some of these comfort zone stretching horses became heart work growing me into what's possible for me to become, I began to see how hard it can be to admit that you might be wrong about why they were let go because you get their side of the story for a better understanding of the extenuating circumstances around a particularly unfortunate dilemma.

As for difficult horses, when we can to not lock them up to how we met them, we're able to listen to why they're behaving in ways that are not safe, or sound, then room for growth is created because we allow them to help us try and make sense of their reason for saying no without the fear of being forced into a yes. Horses don't stay in their body when horses don't feel safe inside their bodies.

That said, bullies have frequently been bullied themselves, but when you're on the receiving end of the wounding, what is done stays with you for years and years, like an ugly scar. Those people who've given themselves permission to do whatever they want to whomever they can by creating a realty for the ones they think they're smarter than is where all my personal horses came from. They ended up with me because they'd turned into the people that had hurt them, which was more than the people who'd hurt them could handle.

The other day, while I was walking with Yoda-pony around the farm, following my breath, a childhood memory appeared in my mind of an old woman in church with her hands raised, head shaking from left to right, face frowned like she smelled something foul. She had tears in her eyes as she listened to the choir of crystal-voiced angels sing magical incantations of ancestral code-song rooted in the alchemical wisdom of enslaved people. People freeing themselves from the fear of yesterday being passed down to the fear of tomorrow by camouflaging suffering in safety and calling that false consciousness fate.

Trying to heal, while trying to grieve, while trying to live, while trying to dream, while trying to smile, while trying to love and be loved is like praying for what's next for you. Receiving answers to prayers you didn't pray about the world tomorrow. Things grow into what they are: I've been saved by the beauty of the horse. So far, in my life with them, I've learned that the biggest killer of relationships comes from not being willing or able to comprehend someone else's point of view, which results in things and people getting broken.

When I can do time a day at a time… or an hour… or a minute… whatever it takes to get through to the space that is life, then nothing is sacred but life, and I'm helpful. So far, I've learned that the more space I leave for life, the more room I have for the spirit. Horses are the spirit of heaven in my heart. Heaven is the place where broken things go to be made as unbroken as possible, again. Horses are bringing me to a different place in my heart, deeper, where nothing but life is sacred. Horses have a beautiful way of helping the heart clarify the soul. And if I said I'm doing everything I just talked about at the same time, all of the time, that would be a lie. Change is each and every single step between then and now. Everything is only one thing.

3]

What my rescues and throwaways have taught me: rejection is a part of service; if you have anybody who really gets you, you are truly blessed (and so are they); how easy it is to send away what you can't help; how you can only receive what you respect; and how hard change really is. Slow and steady instead of all or nothing.

Let's take my mare Mohawk, who was bred to run as fast as her legs could fly. For one reason or another, didn't live up to the expectation of her intended use. When she failed to fly high enough, she was fired.

It's important for me to not forget this scientific fact out of fear of ruining the magic of Mohawk's being-ness. She teaches me how miracles are made out of learning to allow each moment to open your heart a little bit more to the possibility that, sometimes, finding the answer isn't as hard as accepting the answer that you've found. Making something beautiful out of this, like Earth in knowing when you serve those who are overlooked, you serve everyone.

It's taken me nearly three years of allowing Mohawk the space to become an actual horse, learning how to safely express internalized anger at her past instead of continuing as a dissociated survivor of people who got what they wanted, but didn't want what they got after adopting her as a cheap, off the track, three-year-old, flaming red hot chili pepper as a first horse for their thirteen year-old-daughter. A phase in Mohawk's life that taught her how hard it is to be good when you experience how unimaginably bad life can actually be.

When she arrived at my barn, working with Mohawk was like trying to successfully navigate the maze of riddles that the modernization of a big city's new road system by someone who moved away and is visiting from out of town a few years later: a lot of highways with new exits, a lot of detours, a lot of quick changes, making it hard to get off the highway on to the toll road because everything is all twisted up. And you kind of have to know which lane to get in before you get in it. And sometimes your GPS talks too slow: it'll tell you to turn, and there's no turn there.

Some kind of way you sometimes end up where you don't want to be, and you have to move over to the left lane quickly, because you're about to miss your exit. And you look in your rear view mirror, and you don't see anyone driving up behind you before you make a rapid turn, and you hear a horn blow, and they call you a really bad name, and you take it because you looked in your rearview mirror, and your side mirror, but the car behind you was so close up on you that it was in your blind spot.

I think that when we feel safe, and clear, enough to just say what happened, the meaning of this knot the has to be untied becomes that no one makes it out damage free: we suffer from what we participate in. Then, maybe, the purpose of helping others becomes for us to learn to heal ourselves beyond the selfish attachment to energy that causes being put back together again to hurt more than the pain of being broken in the first place. Breathing deeply, and mindfully, into the feeling of feeling trapped inside of a body that can experience so many things in so many nuanced ways is teaching me how to find the courage to not use my horses as an escape from the world hoping for peace. Breathing deeply, and mindfully, into the feeling of being okay with having no idea about what's going to happen is how my horses are teaching me to be present in the world.

Mohawk's getting better every day. This morning, while cleaning her stall, I began thinking about, as I often do, how much of my humanity horses hold... how much of my myself I'm able to find in my life with them. How they see me as I am. As I stood focusing on my breath while I picked through shavings, swept the dirty shavings into little piles, and shoveled those little piles into the muck bucket, Mohawk looked at me, softened her eyes, licked-and-chewed, let out a long sigh, then yawned five times before going back to munching on hay from her hay bag.

4]

I wanted to share a story about one of my horses who, last Wednesday, was being prepared for her lesson by her person. Her person went to brush her around the girth area and the horse began to squeal. This is not normal behavior for this mare. Everybody's first thought was ulcers. She did not have ulcers. She had been taken to the veterinary clinic two weeks ago to be scoped for ulcers and have her Fall checkup. They didn't find anything.

The doctor came out to my barn last Friday. It was a new veterinarian because her regular vet couldn't come. It was a new vet and they sent a student vet, so each veterinarian had a tech with them. They had looked at the mare's file before they came and decided they were gonna do a lameness exam. I said she wasn't presenting as lame, and it didn't really make sense to me why we would be doing that. If anything, maybe a chiropractic adjustment was needed: her front legs are uneven because of a ligament snip she'd had when she was a baby. She was born with a club foot.

I'm saying this not to bash anybody: I don't tell stories to bash veterinarians just like I don't tell stories to bash trainers. I tell stories to share some of my experiences of being shown over-and-over again that energy flows where the mind goes. How, when we're able to combine what we know with how feel, we're able to understand how the limits of our awareness also become the limits of our ability to tune into that in-between space. This space is where creation is an information ocean, opening minds wide so our eyes can see what oneness means: not looking away until you discover a sincere friend staring back at you from the reflection in the mirror. The miracle of your heart no longer feeling like an old house full of pale prayers with no ground for being and just the tiniest pinprick of light inside of it.

Anyway, the veterinarian asked me to lunge the mare. The mare doesn't do well on the lunge when heavy winds are blowing because they make my arena scream like a banshee, and that sound scares her. So I rode her instead, and the vet said,

"Well, she's a little lame on the front left."
I was like, "Well, the front left is her shorter leg, and she needs about twenty minutes to warm up, then she's good to go."

Eventually, it was agreed upon that an ultrasound would be our best next step. So, we take the mare into the wash bay and do the ultrasound. On the left side of her body, she's fine. She starts getting agitated on the right side of her body, towards the back of the ribs and more towards the lumbar spine.

I said, "The mare is talking."

The vet said, "Oh, it's just behavior. She's getting impatient. We can sedate her if you want."

By this time, the mare was showing her teeth and putting her ears back, and the tech shanked her with the lead rope. I said, "No." I said, "Right there." The vet stopped at her liver, looked at her computer screen, and said, "This is not normal." She said, "White spots are showing up on the ultrasound on her liver." They looked like little diamonds. As soon as the vet acknowledged that, the mare took a deep breath and relaxed. Then the vet moved a little bit further down her rib cage, towards the middle of her barrel, and there were also little diamonds on her kidney. So they took a blood draw.

On Tuesday, when the vet came back to biopsy a lump in the mare's girth area, I thanked her for taking the time and being willing to listen to the little grey mare's communication during the ultrasound last week. The vet smiled and said, "Thank you for knowing her well enough to be able to put words to her behaviors for me." She said, "Behavior is really tricky."

5]

I've had horses arrive at my barn which, if they were a person, would, I imagine, be a ward of the state living the rest of their lives in a government-run mental institution. Most of the crazy horses I've confronted weren't, but the situations they've come from were. They had to learn to be a lion shielding the lamb they really are with the anger-mask love often wears to keep from being misused.

These horses have taught me that what we call resistance is them protecting themselves from being at the mercy of people who, for one reason or another, they don't feel have their best interest at heart. And the fact that those types of horses have been conditioned to expect a power dynamic to show up during a schooling session, or while getting their feet worked on by the farrier, or at feeding time, or while leading them to the field to play with their friends is still mind-boggling to me.

It's a beautiful act to help a horse's love overshadow its hurtful memory-fueling anger enough to give people another chance at being a helpful friend. I've had some of these horses start breaking out in confrontational behavior, who, because I wouldn't engage with them in equally confrontational behavior, would be at a loss for my lack of warlike-ness and try to attack me. Because that's how they are used to getting attention from the people in their lives who punished them for what they got wrong instead of praising them for what they got right.

Also, we cannot help the hurt horse heal by imitating the people who hurt the horse in the first place. That said, it's a scary thing, being a trainer trying to prove yourself worthy of the money people pay you to "fix" their really difficult horses when you need the money that you're trying to prove yourself worthy of by forcing the answer too soon.

I've seen the implacable expectation of a 30, or 60, or 90 day miracle extinguish the art and the drive of people from being better helpers of horses. They couldn't afford to see how you respond is determined by how you feel on any given day and how after your bad mood changes, it's still possible for an ill-tempered, split-second answer to live forever.

I've had people bring horses to me with major training challenges that they have struggled with for years, and I've been able to literally fix the problem in five minutes with a little minor adjustment. On the opposite end, I have one horse who'll be leaving at the end of the month, but whose mind I've been unknotting for eight years. Ever since I've been home from my travels abroad, I've been guiding him through that space of learning to let go of the stories that are no longer useful. And he has! Now he and his person begin the next part of their journey together. I'm thankful.

That chronic inability to take the time it takes, for whatever reason, as the easiest way of working with horses is a dead end. Horses have time. People usually don't have time, but horses do, indeed, have all the time it takes. This is one of the main reasons I do rehab: the inner freedom to realize what's realizable, like how a horse can't progress any faster than the damage has healed. And also, how hard patience is before you understand that slow is fast, and how brilliantly your compassion can make on horses who have been given up still possible for themselves again.

That said, for me, when it comes to working with horses, compassion (which is not a lack of healthy and fair boundaries) means the courage to be opened hearted and present enough to breathe deeply into your body. To see what's going on in your mind, observe your clarity, your side of mutual consideration, calm and life-affirming creativity. By not moving beyond where relaxation is possible so that you're as safe in a space as possible for the horses to trust that they have a voice that's heard, and listened to in their life and work with your heart.

I think it's also important to remember not to hold the human race hostage for people learning to become human beings. I, personally, am thankful for being able to change, learn to practice better, and let go of what's no longer helpful. I'm still growing...

6]

For me, these last few months of mostly glum funk have been like a book with pages I wish I could tear out and write new ones in their place. It's felt like a long drought with no sign of rain. First, it was scary, then it hurt, then it didn't matter anymore that the night had become so much harder than the day that I'd begun to curse the darkness instead of light a candle. When I realized I'd reached that point, I gave my horses time off from our work together because my heart had obviously become too heavy a weight for them to carry.

And so I re-awakened my evening practice of sitting on my meditation mat and following the breath deep down into the orange glow of my belly, where healing is like an angel waiting to guide me on my journey to truth, when I'm not afraid to let go of what I once held as true. Breath is the sign that life still needs bodies for beings to be able to learn and teach.

It had taken me some time to find my way back to that place because I'd been left a little off balance after that big kerfuffle with the cunning clan of hungry ghosts. But, once I reestablished my connection to my heart, I could relax enough to take an honest look at the role I was playing in my suffering.

There were mornings when I observed my lawyer-self trying to convince my jury-self that the war for peace between wants and needs is actually one of the most precious gifts of love by saying, "Nothing is perfect. Even if something was perfect, it would be your idea of perfect and not mine. A really beautiful part of being conscious and capable of feeling is giving space for yourself not to be perfect. You'll fail to remember some things. I'll say something that will be misunderstood. I'm not giving you a hall pass but rather holding on to our connectedness, even in those spaces where we're not perfect. Those canyons of imperfection are the bridge that connects worlds. When you act like everything is always OK, you're left fighting your battles alone. That connection is where help is found."

As I continued listening to how I was using fear as license to drive people away who were truly trying to help me, I found myself in the middle of a memory about a horse who had acted like his amygdala had been hijacked by the recollection of too many methods that were big on time and little on relationship. All of the programs he'd been in, he'd flunked out of for being untrainable.

When his person called me, she'd shared how when she picked him up from the last trainer he was at, he had a body score of two, his hooves hadn't been kept up, and how she'd brought him back to health. He hadn't been ridden in quite a while and he was usually spooky and had a big buck. As soon as I saw him, I knew he would soften if I could help him feel considered, heard, and listened to. So, I gave him a treat, asked for his lead rope, and introduced myself to him as I showed him around my arena.

After he was saddled, she put his bridle on, which caused his body to become tense and stone-like: his brows furrowed, he braced his neck and inverted his back, the corners of his mouth also got crinkly, and his eyes were blank. His bridle bit seemed to be a trigger that reminded him of what had happened and made him afraid of what could happen again. It's hard to have the peace of where you are always being assassinated by the threat of where you've been. But, I think life gives us an understanding in the places we didn't have understanding before. Like learning how to turn hardship into headway before choosing again and moving on; how emotions can make you believe, then disbelieve, then becomes an enemy of what you once believed. How choices are magic things that linger; how to win by not playing when possible, and how there's nothing more powerful than a changed mind.

That said, I define grace as the good gifts we find freely, what we love and find peace in. That's the meaning I take hold of and run with when I struggle to be thankful for the unblocking of hearts that being a student of the horse is. We change because of the distance between here and there. I'm still growing into the human I'd want to be if I was one of the horses in my world by learning to stay more receptive to where their questions come from and why they ask them.

The speaker leaving room for the listener to respond is the awareness of the mind within itself and the world, which is the essence of true connection. So, I switched him to a bit that gave his tongue more relief, after which he took a deep breath, blinked deeply, and lowered his head. Then he licked and chewed. I rode him with no problem after that. He was soft, quiet, and calm.

7]

When I'm about to grow, and a big change is about to happen in my life, a shift, I always become physically weak to the point of being nearly stuck on my mattress. The last time I had this dream it wasn't a dream. I couldn't sleep, and so I sat up in bed. We have a chakra, an energy center, right at the base of our skull, and that little center opened up. With my awareness, I just walked right in, and it was so incredible to see the inside of myself.

I saw my mind working in my body, and I saw my mind in my blood. I watched the backs of my eyelids close and open over my pupils. I could stand at the edge of my nasal cavity and look down my nostrils at the brown vermillion border of my top lip.

It was weird and so cool to see my body working and I saw my mind in all of it. I have never experienced anything like that before. Then I went to sleep for a few hours, and I woke up, I was good as new.

When I follow a thought out of present moment emptiness, I become a thought of the future or the past, and I'm no longer able to feel. Feel is how I've learned to be responsible for the energy I bring to horses, people, and my trust in life—even when it doesn't feel good. When I follow thought I become thought lost in the ego. Ego is the ghost of the thinker's thoughts. Ego is every prayer I've ever prayed except, "Thank you."

Ego is what some people, who want you to be the answer to the question that they, in fact, are the answer to, use to try and rob you of your being human-ness by putting you on a pedestal because of their need to have a pet to worship like a highly prized Buddha statue, only to turn around and try to knock you down, like a dynamited building, for not being what you never said you were in the first place. And what a waste of time, especially since reality is what's left after all the imagined things have melted away like the clocks in Dalí's *Persistence of Memory*. Time is the brain.

I'm able to find heaven in every step when I follow horses because horses are miracles from heaven, manifesting things in me that I didn't think were there in those preciously unpleasant, meaning-of-life moments that I wish were picture perfect. Hardship has a way of giving clarity and insight into the health of your heart and mind that you didn't have before.

I'm just a simple horseman trying to listen to horses enough to help them with their humans when their humans bring them to me for help. That said, it sometimes feels like it would be too good to be true if no one had to be set on fire to keep others warm. How much more healed would the whole world be if that mystery was revealed to everyone? I often wonder.

Until then, I'm slowly becoming a better human for my horses and for myself. Other humans and the earth, too, by continuing to cultivate a love that's wide enough to allow for growth and change in love and truth. Like a tree, beyond the holding of a self-image that tries to keep me from the fact that I'm floret-ing into deeper-and-deeper states of knowing.

And what a gift: to try and help others also find that breath-filled space within light-filled space where "I" becomes "we" becomes "you," exchanging perseverations for the contentment that the senses romp around inside of like happy horses playing in the field of letting go. Horses are the light leading my light back to its light. The question is the answer.

8]

My arena is my safe place, like a hermitage, or a meditation hall, where I go to think about definitions as the offspring of concentration and craft and the dictionary as an epic poem about people needing to create worlds out of meaningful language for what we all feel, but don't really always know how to express; and about how maybe the purpose of this journey is to realize how long the road to good intentions really is.

My arena is like a wish dragon who appears when I try to make progress without anyone else knowing about it, out of fear of calling too much of other people's awareness to myself showing up for myself so that I can show up for whomever else I'm able to when I'm teaching, like my very reliable friendship with good poetry and beautiful music, where there is room for every feeling to be safely felt so that I know what each feeling means to me in my hope for honest attention beyond the transactional, like my now four-year-old oldest niece who always wants to talk about her entire existence before bedtime because she doesn't want to fall asleep, yet.

I love teaching. It allows me to practice being open to how others hear so that I can be helpful, because connection is communication, which has given me tools to help me prevent myself from going so far inside myself that I don't come back. Like the star I saw falling through the night sky from outer space earlier this morning on my way down to the barn to do my chores. It happened right before driving up to Boulder to work with the students in my Second Sunday Lesson Group. But I also know that things take time. So, I'm taking as much as I can.

And this is what taking the time it takes with a horse looks like in the inside of my mind when I take it: being human is hard work, especially that part about inter-being, in a reduced down, non-tribal, one-on-one sort of way; and how we have to give up so much out of our love for them. How that love can change us so much that we find the courage to conquer our impulse of doing the worst thing we can do: turning them into ourselves, and thus working so hard to give them what they don't really need from us. Humans being with horses is not a game of "us" versus "them" where the winner is the one who succeeds in taking the other's choices away the most.

The only voice I have for other people to hear is the healing song of horses holding space for me. At the same time, I listen to a rider's energy flow with my body so that, hopefully, I guide him or her or them through the process of relaxing their body language and movement enough to be able to follow the horse's back with the seat bones and the horse's hind legs with the hands. Sound moves the spirit by changing the atmosphere. There are so many layers to this onion.

If it's possible that the only real lesson horses have to teach humans is that we can't create trust with chaos, then how much do you think your forgiveness would cost if you were your horse? I think about this often, all of the mistakes I've made. If different outlooks lead to different outcomes, what else is there to do but see what can be seen and become like a lotus flower blossoming in sunlight? The quest to understand the question is the answer. Life survives on the right questions being asked. That said, you have to be emotionally safe to put words to feelings. And even though we are all in the space between each other, I'm still an immigrant in my field of dreams.

I listen to horses and their people as if I'm sitting in the audience of Nina Simone's 1976 concert at the Montreux Jazz Festival as she sings about Mr. Backlash: how he's there every day and is always the same; and how his story is one of needing to forget feeling good about being able to break all of the rules and still win and how art lives in his story. How his story lives in art and how art is trust in the good. How the good is only part of her story about memories that she refuses to forget.

I listen to horses and their people as if I'm sitting in the audience of Nina Simone's 1976 concert at the Montreux Jazz Festival as she sings *Feelings*: not knowing if I'm being driven off the side of a cliff into a canyon or led up to the mountain peak of loose, salacious mercy. A place where miracles are like long blades of grass in a beautiful hay field, reminding me how every breath is always the most all-embracing truth, second only to the earth, that we all have access to. When I don't know what to say, my mind always thinks everything, so I focus on breathing in-and-out until my thoughts slow down enough for the inside of my mind to feel like a familiar spirit again. The breath is always the beginning...

I listen to horses and their people as if I'm sitting in the audience of Nina Simon's 1976 concert at the Montreal Jazz Festival as she sings *I Wish I Knew How It Would Feel To Be Free*, thinking about how the beginning of wisdom is knowing when what once worked doesn't work anymore and how very real the struggle is. How beautiful the work.

9]

And this is the thing about a good story. They're everywhere if you're interested enough to pay attention to what is being said or not. This has been the enchantment of reading a well-written piece of literature for me ever since I was a little boy.

Still, to this day, I talk to my books out loud sometimes. I ask them questions, then put my ear to the words on the page and listen for any sort of acknowledgment from them. Sometimes I get one. Sometimes not, just like with horses. This listening practice is how my voice learned to walk across words like a bridge with a free-footed seeker just on their way to comprehending that the answer is the question and that the question is a praise.

Horses have taught me how to see movement as a powerful treasure to be honored with little glories, and quiet rituals, and simple routines of support, safekeeping, and care beyond the religion of traditional method-like things that are so full of where you came from, but at the cost of where you are right now, and where you could go if only the possibility of what-if's were allowed to sing Mercy. That said, the basics are all there is. They are the best "only" shot a horse has of surviving in our fast-forward world of forgetting how to crawl before you walk, walking before you run, and running before you fly.

I don't know, for sure, if there's an all-knowing, unseen force guru-ing me along this path. Still, I do believe it with my whole heart because it helps me find peace, and not feel so lost. Alone in this chaotic, loud, jangly world when I go out into it to try and understand how to best be of service, and not be so socially awkward around outside people and still feel safe enough to be vulnerable inside of this little man's body, I'm living in at the moment. It's such a weird experience, this guy's journey. The lease will be up soon enough, I suppose.

What I do know, though, is that time is the red ball of yarn that my younger calico cat, Eva, likes to chase across that Navajo rug on our bathroom floor like a mouse; and that paying as close attention as I can to how my horses change with every encounter I experience with them is progress; and that staying mindful of how my soul is doing in getting a better understanding of itself by following the breath into those buried-alive emotions that trauma hides inside of like a drop of blood flowing through my veins is helping heal pupal staged ancestors cocooned inside of the woven silk of generations to come, which has given me the courage to not be as afraid to speak publicly in the language of light like dark night stars softly singing early in the morning, before the sun re-wakens the sky from its rest, again.

And this is what I've learned so far: everything is. The word "is" means "to be." To be is the practice of being. Being is the art of *Is*. *Is* is our spirit. For me, each one of our spirits is like a dendrite, those short-armed tree branch-like extensions of a nerve cell, receiving little electrical tingles of enlightenment, and imagination, and motivation from its latticework of lifetimes sculpting a future out of what our brains have built for us to live inside of, like my two and four year old nieces gleefully carousel-ing around their giant sandbox, with its aqua colored kick-boards, like ecstatic little whirling dervishes dancing on the front porch of heaven to the heart-opening underwater recordings of blue whale ocean songs when the horses aren't working. Energy follows thought.

What we think and how we think it, and with whom, all determine who the horse is hearing speak when they open our energy up. Like a collection of poems as the pages are read. The pages of balladry in search of a survivable distance as possible from which to observe us, not realizing that we can't relax our bodies any deeper than we're willing to breathe into our bodies. Study if the meaning for having horses in our lives is thickly layered and out of harm's way, enough for horses to lay down inside and find some rest.

All that to say that who we are with, and for, and because of, and in-spite of ourselves is the heart of our connection with horses. This connection is the heart of our partnership with horses, out of which the "how" we do what we do with horses is rooted. What a powerful, beautiful, amazing gift

9)

and opportunity to learn and grow…

This evening, I looked up and saw the very beautiful and brightly shining, Venus, beside the waxing crescent moon like a doula ushering a infant in from the embryonic ocean of dreams when I conjured up the conversation with my mom while we were preparing our horses for bed about what I'd learned from the riding lessons with my students a few hours earlier in the day.

10]

I'd missed my exit and got lost yesterday morning on my drive up north to Wellington to teach my Fourth Sunday Group, even though I had Google Maps. How do you have someone talking to you and a map right in front of you and still miss your exit? My turn came too soon. For a second, I couldn't figure out how someone could have so much to help us navigate and still get off track. But I did.

I was far away in my thought-garden, trying to figure out the reason so many people fight so hard to not say yes to the honest-to-goodness answer staring back at them. Offering to guide them each and every step of the way to the matching question and how to ask it. Like a puzzle when it starts to become a beautiful image of a meadowlark on a wire instead of just a gazillion little separate pieces spread out of the dining room table.

How in yoga, one way to teach a stiff-backed person to do a standing forward bend is with a one-thousand-count ream of paper. If the teacher takes away a sheet a day, the student's fingertips will safely touch the floor soon enough. When we're addicted to outcomes, it seems like a lot. When we're not, it's just part of the process.

10)

I ended up in Broomfield, and thank goodness the possibility of human error was built into the navigation system so that it could know where I was lost. The computer re-calibrated itself around my wandering hermit of a mind and told me: Form where you are now; you'll need to do this to get back on track. So, I made a right turn onto Baseline Road. From there, it took me to I-25, and I was, thankfully, able to get to my first lesson on time at nine.

This is kinda how I work with horses who want my help to feel better in themselves. They lead me to the answer like those magical heart whispers my mom always tells me are the angels lighting my way.

11]

Yesterday at a clinic, after I got off of one of my client's horses, she said, "It just looks so effortless when you do it. I wish I could ride like that. Everything always seems right when you do it, and I can't ever seem to find that place of oneness. I just wish I could..." I told her, "The closer you are, the further away you feel." That's the mystery of silence.

I'd woken up from a dream a few days ago. A swan with a slim, elegantly arched neck and milky-tipped poppy-colored beak floated along the light that passes through the realm of all living things. A black, feathery storm cloud across the sky while its webbed feet paddled beneath the surface like two gently rowing oars. The light was all of those who've ever been loved, or will ever be loved to help whoever can be nurtured back to harmony with themselves so that, once cured, they can help someone else get whole, too. We'd be there together again like before. We were exited into love by the Higgs-like particle that triggered this articulation about why people working towards clarity with horses is so important to me.

I told her:
 I just want to be a horseman in my heart, you know, in the

truest sense of the word, beyond where everyone thinks horses are, or what horses are, as defined by those who've given us those definitions, to what horses actually are, and where horses actually are. Experience can't be defined—and when we have an experience all that's left for us to do is be who and what we are while we have the time. Being with horses is more than delegating them to a trained response. Horses are more than that, so are people.

I told her:
I often don't know whether I'm going or coming half the time. I don't know what I am: when I'm training, I'm trying to learn all that my horses want to teach me. I feel like a student. When I'm teaching, I'm trying to share what I've been able to learn from my horses, which sometimes feels like nothing... It's easy to mistake what's written in a book about working with horses for what's actually being said because horses can still speak to us on more levels than we can read, see, hear, or understand. But, we only know what's being said by first knowing what's already been said. The future is made of the past. It is always predicated by what was.

I told her:
And so the question remains; how can we expect horses to be everything we want them to be if we're not willing to be what they need us to be for them to be what we want them to be? For me, when I watch you ride, your horse is a map of your mind with all of its mind-things wondering about my perceptions of you as a rider, if I have what it takes to

make what I'm teaching applicable to you, and if you have what it takes to follow me as far as you're hoping I can lead you. For me, as a teacher, all of these things are a gift...an invitation to grow beyond the paralysis of fear. And this is the thing about a gift, we don't know what we've been given if we don't take off the wrapping paper. With horses like yours, our greatest gifts are often wrapped up in their problems, which is usually them just answering the question they hear us asking instead of the question we'd intended to ask.

By the end of the lesson, she had changed the angle of her ischia towards the front of the saddle by lifting her heels a little so that she could better follow her horse's now beautifully lifted back with her seat and feel his swinging hind legs in her hands. On the drive home, I imagined the faded blood-stained cement walls, the faded blood-stained cement floor with a drain in the middle, and a huge rusty hook that hung from the heavy chain dangling down from the rail that allowed for slaughtered carcasses to move around with relatively little hassle. I'm doing the best I can to try and help fewer horses suffer that fate.

12]

This morning, I walked into the arena thinking about my now much less afraid Yoda-pony. How relaxation, the releasing of the body from the reality of stress so that you can be led, is the heart of healthy communication. Whose life-blood is the connecting energy of love when I saw a garter snake serpentining in the soft, warm sand across the centerline.

And like an old sagely cottonwood tree whose earth worming roots have tunneled down deep enough to reach water, I stood, planted, and found myself contemplating how my common sense says: leave the crazy rescue horses alone. But my love won't let them go. For me, the rescue horse is like someone who is outwardly in prison but inwardly free, writing a letter to someone who is outwardly free (but whose heart is not) about compassion being the work of inter-being. How life-nourishing boundaries are the keepers of sanity and how not allowing love to have loopholes is a candle flame honoring the light in a dark room. How searching for connection with horses is the pain I feel when I get lost in the belief that I'm separate from love and how the structured practice of daily routine is the maker of miracles. How trouble doesn't always last, but sometimes, trauma stays a while, like a flood after the storm that caused it to run out of rain. Like taking a hundred years for wetlands to fully heal after the submarine pipeline from which the oil spilled was capped, and how forgiveness isn't always another chance at trust. How love is not love without an object to love, even if it's from a distance for a while because any closer at the moment isn't healthy. Love allows you to leave and come back better, holds space for the possibility of a chance to grow, and doesn't limit you to how it met you. It's our only human hope, I think.

Anyway, for one reason or another, that glittering little black-and-silver slithering friend triggered the memory of the time I was in Crestone, Colorado, when I first learned how to go back into those parts of my past that I needed to heal for my future. After that experience was over, it was late in the evening, and I was afraid to go to sleep because earlier, when I opened the front door to the house to get my duffle bag out of my car, there were all of these wide, round, slowly blinking eyes looking out at me from the forest.

I saw a mosh pit like throng of shadowy hands reaching up from the living room floor, promising to pull me through if I laid down, once I returned inside the house. This is what happens to me, sometimes, when answers come: I get taken to another place. There was a Book of Common Prayer on the living room bookshelf. I read the whole book aloud, then told myself: "You have to get some sleep, but you will wake up in the morning." Then I had a dream. In it, an angel-man named Boone.

12)

Crestone is in the Valley of Peace, where all the First Nations tribes of the region would gather, before reservations, to do their diplomacy. In the summertime, when you look up, the clouds sometimes look like a herd of steeplechasers jumping a ditch. In the dream, Boone and I were at the foot of Mt. Crestone, which to me looks like head of a lady wearing a beautiful hat (a beautiful wide-brimmed, oversized Kentucky Derby hat). I told him about the vision I had when I opened my acceptance letter for graduate school: how there was a bullet being shot into my brain from the barrel of a gun up against the side of my head, just above my right ear. I didn't know what it meant or what to do with it, so I took a gap year. Boone asked if that's how I wanted my story to end.

I said, "No."

He said, "Then give it to the clouds."

By this time, Boone and I had floated up to the peak like bubbles on their way to the surface. And there I was, in the center of this mountain lady's elegant hat with this angel-man, my open-palmed hands raised skyward, praise-like, feeling this part of the story leave my body like a soul being guided to the light.

Instead of completing my graduate studies, I traveled abroad for a few years to practice following the signs. The last place I lived overseas was a city in China, approximately two hours north of Shanghai by train, called Wuxi. I had a condo on the sixteenth floor with a balcony looking out over the polluted Yellow River.

Late one night, my sister called because my great-grandma, Big Mom, who was one-hundred-and-five years old, was dying. My sister handed Big Mom the phone when it was explained to me what was happening. After I said "Hi," Big Mom told me: "Honey, I just wanted to call because I'm walking through my body and turning off all the lights." She said, "This is the last time that you will hear from me here like this." She said, "I just wanted to tell you that I love you, and that I'm proud of you, and that as long as you stay on the road you're on, everything will be just fine…just fine." Then she handed the phone back to my sister. Thirty minutes after the call was over, Big Mom moved upstream to the ancestors. The next day, I quit my job and bought a plane ticket home.

A week after Big Mom's burial, I got a call from one of my former riding instructors at the Urban Farm about a beautiful and brilliantly gifted but broken-bodied (and seemingly glacial-hearted, baby-seal-skin colored), eleven-year-old thoroughbred gelding that had been rescued and given to her, and whose name had been changed from Primo to Nova. The word was out to nearly every up-and-coming professional dressage and jumping trainer in the region about how impossible to work with this horse was.

It was a cold October morning when I went out to meet him. I asked what he thought about the things I'd heard about him and from whom. He stayed silent. When I asked what it was I needed to understand for him to allow me to help him,

12)

Nova said: "For those who have attempted to hold me back, or mistaken my generosity for weakness to be exploited or to hurt me, I let it go. But I wish them upon themselves." The treasure hunt had ended. I'd found my Teacher.

13]

A few months back, I was interviewed about my horsemanship practice by this old Hall of Fame stockman from the Bible Belt who asked how I came up with my name. "I've never heard of it before," he said. "It's not simple like mine. Tell me about that, would you?"

I said:
Sure. My mommy gave me my name after she gave birth to me. She said I came out with one eye open, looking around at where I'd just landed. Nahshon means one who sees. In The Midrash, Nahshon is a prince in the tribe of Judah. He's also included in the genealogy of Jesus Christ at the beginning of the Gospel of Matthew. Why he's so important is because before the children of Israel escaped from six hundred of Egypt's chosen chariots, horsemen, and the rest of Pharaoh's army by Moses, effectively turning the Red Sea into the walls of a hallway while Nahshon walked, head-deep into the water. He initiated the Exodus.

I said:
The future comes from the past; memories, no matter how

long ago, only lead us to the present moment. Time is a fugitive slave with a baby in her belly and a toddler in her arms, the Underground Railroad with Harriet Tubman leading the way to freedom from the pounding hoof sounds of bounty hunting slave drivers on horseback in the distance. It goes quick. Harriet Tubman was Moses.

I said:

Judah means praise. The tribe of Judah were people of thanksgiving. That's what all of this is, my work. It's all a prayer of gratitude for my horses; they are a mystery, much like life. Which, as you know, can be really tough. More about them than I can explain is being revealed every day, which has helped me realize how sometimes, in doing something, you're led to something you didn't even know, and that something was really the whole purpose all along.

I said:

Horses are leading me to freedom. I'm already there. I can feel it in my heart. And this is what I've learned so far: so many people give up on their journey because nobody told them at the beginning that they also had to heal the pain-bodies (all of the traumas, emotions, limiting beliefs, and negative thoughts) they'd inherited from generation, after generation, after generation of lives lived in scary places. Where the fear of going backward keeping you from going forward is very real. This is the number one matter in question I'm confronted with when someone comes to me for help with their horse: that person's past.

I said:

Fear paralyzes people. Fear makes people sabotage themselves by pushing away the people trying to help them. Fear can shut you down. Fear can immobilize you. Fear of failure can make you not try. Fear of falling can make you not climb. Fear of being defeated will make you not fight. I see it every day.

I said.

How do I help people through their fear? I try to teach them how taking deep, full-body, breaths to relax their muscles and minds is a way to start learning how to love themselves first, so that they can truly love and listen to what their horses are trying to tell them. Which, for me, is the beginning of true connection and relationship: empathy, fairness, responsibility, and trust.

At the end of the interview, he asked if there was anything I'd like for him to say a prayer for on my behalf.

I said:

Sure. Culture definitely determines what we think is good. But my faith in healing as a process of restoring wholeness is not absent from my fear of not explaining in a clear enough way for you to truly understand what I'm trying to say. I am trying very hard, though. So, if you could please pray that I have the courage to keep walking my road, I'd appreciate that very much. Thank you.

14]

1)

And that place of deep listening that he's in is only possible because of deep relaxation. You feel like this space is a safe enough space for you to be a safe enough space for him, and he is showing that. For me, this is where the training of a horse starts; it has absolutely nothing to do with how they move. It has everything to do with the place from which they move. If a horse is not relaxed in their work, the work is not real.

What I want you to do is conjure the color that makes you feel the safest, and just think about it. Now, with that thought, I want you to allow that color to make you be safe. Sometimes, safety feels tight. Sometimes it's cold, when we conjure it like that. So warm it up, let it get loose. Yes, you first.

See what I mean? You become the safe space, and I think that's the magic of it… That's the miracle of it… You become what you see. Then, you are out of that space. And then, like we talked about yesterday, when you do it for you first, you are that for the people that you're helping. This is what it feels like.

"I can sense it all around. I'm marinating in it."

"Yeah."

And you see, then, that the sharing of knowledge can only come from relationship… It can only come from relationship, and this is how horses are so wise. They're like, "The more detached from fantasy of unhealthy expectations you are, the less unwilling you are to feel. The less unwilling you are to feel, the more clearly authentic you are. The more clearly authentic you are, the more truthfully connected you are." For me, connection is not control. With horses, being more devoted the process than the dream is the bridge between short-term behavioral magmatism and long-term emotional development that makes the fruition of the dream possible.

"This may seem sort of random, but the Statue of Liberty just popped up in my mind. More as an emblem of feminine protection. It's more roundabout than protection in the masculine sense of being strong."

"How does that feel?"

"In alignment."

"Good. Let's go the other direction."

This is the magic of horses. And I want you to ride out of that all encompassing-ness, out of that hug. Out of that warm feeling from the color that makes you feel safe. And when we come into that tension in his body, I want you to feel it, and I want you to surround it with that feeling of safety, and see if we can loosen him with our intention. Which is basically a way of saying, "Don't be afraid to open your heart."

Good, and when he's ready, trot, as an invitation, and just

let it be small. Good, give him your seat: try and relax your quadriceps… soften the toes… there. Yeah. Think it. Feel it. Good. Now, in that Statue of Liberty space that you found, try and half-halt by first opening, then softly lifting your heart to the ceiling. Yeah, now release it. Good! You're so much softer in your position today. Your mind is so much softer. Now we're really beginning to see that the true language of horses is intention. And how freedom is defined by having boundaries that help you feel safe enough to listen, so that we can learn to trust.

Softness is not a boundary-less space. Motherhood is not a boundary-less land, they're just spacious: My mom bought me this farm. And because she got it for me, I know it's a space that I'm safe inside of. I'm free with-in the parameters of this space.

"That's what parents do for their children."
"And this is also how we ride horses in true lightness."
"Yep."
"Unfortunately, so many of our training methods are based taking what we feel entitled to take without the horse's permission…
"We had a practice when our kids were younger, and we got to make those decisions: whenever they asked for something, how could we say 'yes' to them…in a way that they could learn by heart what 'yes' meant."
"Yes."
"So that 'yes' also had boundaries."

"Yes, that's how we ride, and train: these are the parameters, and these parameters are there out of a whole bunch of consideration for you to find the joy in becoming more of yourself? How does it feel?"

"*Liberating.*"

That's why I just hang out with my horses during turnout: I study what they do and how they move when they're able to have total trust in what their bodies are doing in love with the earth while dancing across it in beautifully balletic balance, most of the time. And then, I try in find ways of how I can prove that I'm worthy of a place inside of that space of movement-freedom with them: "How can I get you comfortable enough in my hands for you to dance like that with me?" And when they're doing this with each other, you realize it's because they're in relationship with each other. They are having a conversation: "This is how what you're asking me to do is making me feel?" I want to be there.

It's interesting, how you said you didn't want to ride out of that colonial mindset, it's because you not trying to teach him out of entitlement to his body. You don't feel like it's something for you to take a way from him. And because you don't feel like his body is something you have the right to take from him, he doesn't mind offering it to you.

This is lightness. Lightness has nothing to do with the length of the reins. It has every thing to do with horses wanting to be in relationship with us while ask them questions.

"Some very old and painful memories are coming up…"

"Yeah?"

"And I'm going to tell you this because you have a lot of women students. It can happen to men too, but many of us, women, at one point or another, have had our bodies taken away from us against our will, too. And there are so many… There are walls. Many, many walls…"

"And here again the wisdom of horses: when we see that our need to be in control is out of fear and a protection, we do those things that have been done."

"Or what we would have done if we could have done it."

"I don't think it has anything to do with wishing. I think it has to do with the power I need to protect myself from the hurtful memory of the likelihood of that ever happening to me again. And the question then becomes: do I have the courage to allow myself to be free?"

"…and safe."

"You know?"

"I do."

"And I think that this is the prayer that horses pray for us all of the time: That we have the courage to be honest so that we can embody that ethical responsibility for each other to be authentic enough to be present and feel what we're feeling."

"That went through. I feel clear."

"You look clear."

"Yeah, I needed to release that."

"And as you did, your horse started to relax. They are embodiments of our minds."

"And it doesn't have to linger…"

"In this moment, you decided the power you were going to give it. And I think that that is the important thing: you decide how you will be with it by knowing that the power it has is only there because of the permission you give it to be there."

"Without trying to stop it."

"There's no need to. Observe it. A flower can't take root without soil. Now you have really understood what non-attachment is. It doesn't mean that sexual abuse didn't happen. It just means that it doesn't hurt you anymore."

"That it can just walk by."

"Yeah, like a passing thought through the mind in meditation… And it doesn't mean that you wish that it didn't happen. It just means that it has no power over you anymore."

"I'd like to try and work with him some more before our lesson ends. But I'll let that pass through."

"Let's do this: let's stop for now, and we'll do it again at one o'clock. This was really important. Super. Super."

"I'm just going to ride him around the arena one more time."

"Take the time you need. Take the time you need. Take the time you need. This space is big enough for many people."

"How many?"

"Many."

2)

One of the times it happened to me was when I was living in Thailand. I was twenty-seven. And I don't know for sure how she'd heard about me. The first time I met her, she'd arrived at the stable with her security detail, who drove a black Mercedes van with a siren on top, behind which she followed in one of her five Porches. She was a very beautiful (maybe 45 or 50-year-old) woman. She was dressed in a black pencil skirt that went down just below her knees, black stilettos, and a starched high-collard white cotton blouse with the first three buttons unfastened. She walked around with an auto sunshade over her head so that her pearl-and-cream skin wouldn't tan. Her lips and fingernails were painted Lotus Rouge.

It was explained to me that she'd insisted on being admitted as one of my students and that her lessons would begin the following day. From the start, she was doting and flirtatious. She would tip me one thousand Baht over my lesson fee. This went on for a few weeks, during which time she kept extending invitations for me to join her for lunch. She said she wanted me to meet some of her friends from work.

Finally, I agreed. It was a Monday. I met them at Fuji Restaurant in Siam Paragon. The friends she wanted me to meet were some of her foreign employees from the US, Canada, and Europe. During the course of the conversation, one of them said that she wanted him to make sure that I knew how well she treated her boys: how she took them on trips and bought them expensive things. When she deemed he'd clearly made that point to her satisfaction, she wanted to know if I'd join her on vacation to the Maldives in two weeks.

On Tuesday, while I was at work on my lunch break, a courier arrived with a gift for me from her. It was a brand new iPhone wrapped in a thick sheet of plushy metallic gold gift wrapping paper and a beautiful plushy metallic gold bow. It was in a beautiful plushy metallic gold gift bag. I sent her a text saying thank you. And since I already knew how addictive taking too much can become and how the past can begin to cost you all that you have, like karma, I never took that phone out of the box.

She asked the lady who scheduled my lessons for our next lesson if she could have a time when no one else was riding. It was evening. Six o'clock. The air smelled like smoke from burning trash. We were in the arena, and Micheal Bolton's *When A Man Loves A Woman* was playing on the cafe's sound system across the small stream. I was tightening the pony's girth when she pressed her chest up against my arm, began groping me, and asked if I had feelings for her like the man in the song. I asked her to stop. I held my breath until she did.

The following evening after work, I was at a bar with some friends when she sent me a text message saying how ungrateful a boy I was. I told her I wasn't going to make myself a prisoner of my body so that she could have her way with me again. She told me that I'd eventually have to grow up and stop being so pure if I was going to have a life worth living in this world.

She told me that her problem was that I had too much of my own money. I told her I hoped she'd have a wonderful, restful trip to the Maldives. I never did get a reply back from her after that.

That same evening, I tried to give the still unopened, plastic-wrapped iPhone box in a fancy gift bag away, for free, to one of my ex-pat friends from Scotland. "Otherwise," I told him, "I was just going to throw it away." He insisted on paying me sixty Baht. The next time I saw him, he told me that same phone fell out of his bag one morning on his way to work and had shattered into a bunch of little bits on the street.

That story reminds me of a time I was in the third grade. I had gotten off the school bus at my bus stop, and there was this man in this old beat-up brown rust bucket of a small hatchback sedan.... He stopped behind the bus, and as the bus pulled off, this person pulled up and asked me to get in the car.

I remember (because it was in front an apartment building across from Fairmount Cemetery on Quebec between Alameda and South Parker Road). I remember moving close to the wood lap rail fence in front of one of the apartment buildings that were there by the road, and he person just kept driving he car closer and closer and closer to me, and opened the passenger door. I remember they had driven so close to me that I could see into the back of the car. The back seat was down. There was an old blue blanket spread out. I ran.

15]

So, in the reframing of this experience, It is us coming upon a place within ourselves that has been there forever, but is now newly born. Where we don't do anything to horses but we do everything for horses, and we don't do to ourselves, but for ourselves, for the purpose of being heard, meaning that I understand, and I acknowledge. I recognize that I have a voice, right? What does that space mean?

For me, it means that there are some stories we have to let go of because they aren't helpful anymore. And so surrendering to the reality that everything you've built your life out of you've mostly outgrown, and it's time to do something else; and how scary that is. But also, how much of a gift being able to be afraid in that situation is. I have a chance to be not who I want but what I want to be. I get to define the parameters in which I am in a world that has been defined for me.

That's what the groundwork with Leo these eight months has been: him being able to define the parameters of how he will be with us in a world in which he is already defined: a foal whose conformation was not worthy of the show ring he was over-bred for. Thankfully, he didn't end up as raw, thin-sliced pieces of cherry blossom meat being dipped in ginger-and-onion-spiced soy sauce at a dinner party in Japan. He's such a sweet-natured dude.

Creating the space in a world that you want to live in. If you don't do that, there's no space to be. What does that mean? For me, the world created for us to be with our horses isn't sufficient for the holiness that lay in that relationship. It's a place where you love your horse enough to let them get old enough to healthily retire when they can't be ridden anymore and not put them to sleep. For me, a horse's value isn't based on human greed. But instead, on being able to see that horses are one of our greatest teachers of lessons we must learn: To stop destroying the earth with our worlds.

It's like this butterfly here who keeps trying to fly through the ceiling. But, because it keeps crashing against the skylight, it keeps falling down to the ground until somebody comes to help and frees us from the illusion of the sky.

> *"Why am I flying up, but I keep falling down?"*
> Because there's a window there.

You're only looking up, and not forward, out in front of you. You're only looking up. You don't see that you're inside of a thing because you're not looking forward at the door. You're looking up to the sky that the door is keeping you away from. And if you find the door, you realize that there's nothing outside keeping your butterfly-self from flying in the sky.

This whole thing is about moving beyond the butterfly crashing into the skylight thinking it's the sky, and how the obligation of someone who sees it is to pick the butterfly up once it's fallen into the hoof-tracked arena indoor sand, and take it outside, so it doesn't have to fall down anymore. One thing following horses has taught me is that I can only help others as much as I'm willing to be aware of myself.

So you've stopped flying up to the ceiling, falling to the floor, and looking forward to the door. Now you have two choices: move ahead and grow, or not. That's where you're at. How you proceed determines what (or if) you will learn. And whatever decision you make is neither good or bad. It's just the decision you're ready for. But also know that this time around, you may not get another chance to walk through that door.

In spite of everything else, the horses in my care know I'm on the earth to give them what they need from me and to try and teach my students to do the same; and in turn, learn to recognize what we, as humans, need to be healthy, too. This is how horses teach us how to heal ourselves. They don't do it for us. They teach us how to do it for ourselves by us truly loving them.

16]

I just had to kill a rattle snake that was facing off with my cat, Ginger, in front of the hay barn. I must admit, I'm sad that I had to do that. I pancaked him with two cinder blocks and chopped his spine in half with the tractor bucket before throwing him in one of the dumpsters that we put the horse manure in. Naturally, that got me thinking about my life with horses and what it all means. I cried and said a prayer for forgiveness. Sometimes, I disappear until I feel like me again.

Breathing is it. I'm learning more and more to use my training sessions as meditation. Training sessions as meditation is just consciously breathing while I work. Breathing in-and-out of the nose doulas the mind deeply into the present moment.

When I'm living from my lungs, I see that the work of the breath is awareness of ourselves and others, connecting us to the world, reaching out by looking in.

When I breathe in through my nose and out of my mouth, I'm trying to re-home stress, with its lifetimes of no peace and fake promises every day, by living from my mind. Mind-living is the land of urgency, brain, and body-at-flight tension.

Mind-living is shallow breathing. When my breath is shallow, it means that my nerves are unsettled. Shallow breathing means I'm thinking about too many things to be flexible in my mind enough to listen, which makes my body tense. Shallow breathing means my mind is not with my horses so my horse's minds can't be with me.

That horses offer themselves to us as a path to self-mastery is truly an incredible gift of grace and light leading us to become more clear with our intentions and questions beyond our paralyzing fear of them. That they teach us how to change, because we are the problem, that is the magic of horses.

This is the yoga of horsehumanship: managing your breath to focus outside of your mind enough to see what the horse sees; which frees you from the burden of yourself.

This has taught me how to let horses decide when they are ready and able to offer the answer to the question. Time and patience and more time and patience when they arrive at my barn abused and scared, or broken and in pain.

One step at a time, the horse will begin to trust again, carefully. The "scars" may never go away completely, but they can be minimized enough for our friends to feel safe. This is the art of choosing conversation instead of debate: being soft, vulnerable, and grateful in each moment for the gift of another chance to breathe again.

The struggle is real. Love is the work.

17]

All right, so, let's ask him to lift the inside shoulder on the circle. Just lift the rein softly. Just lift, there you go. Good. It's all right. Yeah, and once he's there, just let him find it. And with that, we're gonna ask him to just bring his haunches-in, gently: just open your inside heel toward me. There, and keep his inside shoulder lifted wit the inside hand. There and straight. Good job.

Good, let's do it again. Open the inside hand towards me, and gently lift the inside hand. And let's go the other direction. Also, I appreciate you just listening to me talk yesterday. I'm finding my way, you know. Good, lift up on the inside rein gently, and then inside heel open. Now, let him find it. Now, look to me, and doing your chest in my direction. Good, there's your half-pass. Perfect. Just walk around and marinate in that for a minute. Walk around the whole school, that was good.

He's keeping his shoulders up beautifully. Good, let's do it again, here. Lift the inside rein gently, close to his neck and in front of his withers, keep your chest straight, and open your inside heel: we're going to do a haunches-in. Now, just turn your chest slightly in toward me, but keep the rest of your body where it is. Chest over. Chest over, and lift up on the inside rein a little bit. There. There it is. Good.

Good, now we'll play with shoulder-in a bit. And what I want you to do is gently lift the inside rein to get him to lift his inside shoulder and hip, then gently open the inside knee and toe out towards the inside of the arena. Now, open your heel, and let him find you asking him for haunches. Yes, good, and straight. This is a beautiful way of riding. It's soft.

And when you have horses like my young mare, who are so sensitive, they make you find a better way to be. She requires that I keep my mind so slow and listening-ly present. One way that is super helpful for me to practice this is when I do my morning chores with a thirty-five pound weighted vest on for three hours from five to eight, and then I wear five-pound forearm weights. That's my morning routine for creating calm and open-ness for myself for the day.

Good, now let's do haunches-in on the circle. Good, let him find your question. Good, now shoulder-in. Think, outside shoulder in. There you go, good. He likes that... Good man. Very good. My mommy told me something last night on our way to see her cats in the barn. It was so brilliant. She said, "The purpose of a question is to undo what you did to get you back to where you were before you started." For some reason, those words made me think of how belief feels like falling in love, which is only the first step in a life. People are only human when they love a lot.

In this work, the question for me is always, "What is the horse hearing me say?" The horse is affirming that our question is correct when they relax into our asking of it. Essentially, this means we take the question apart to figure out what is not understood, and we clarify that piece of a question within the question. Within this we find the answer that allows us to piece the question back together again to completion.

We're able to keep our ego out of the way because our horses are affirming the work is correct. And it's good when we find the place where he lets us know not only that he can do what we're asking, but that what we're asking feels good. And it's not like some mythical, esoteric practice. But rather a real down-to-earth connection.

You said at the beginning that you wanted to learn how to do the half-pass without contortion. And we realize that when we listen to the contortion our pressure-filled commands turn into, we realize are able to see in the gaps and shadows where the killer of connection is hiding. When we listen into those spaces we're able to hear how, in fact, there's no listening happening at all. Then we go back to the question to undo what you did to get back to where you were before you started: intention. It's like you've said; when a math problem isn't working, sometimes it's more beneficial to erase the whole thing and just start over. Let's try again.

And so now we're going to take the haunches-in and we're going to continue getting his hind end in shape. So, let's do it in the circle. Don't think about it too much, feel it. Gently engage your inside rein again and let your aids be alive. Now halt: open your heels. Haunches-in within the halt. Good. Now, transition to walk in haunches-in. Keep your mind in your belly. Now, mind in your feet: halt. Haunches-in. He likes this. He's dropped.

This is what follow-the-horse and finding heaven in every step feels like. This is that freedom feeling I was talking about yesterday: when I'm riding and when I'm teaching, I'm free because they're affirming that space of openness. You realize that when you don't need to control others you're able to transcend almost every boundary that has been created. It's cool once you get it. It's the most amazing feeling in the world.

When he's ready, track right down that wall in haunches-in. Gently lift the inside rein against his neck in-front of the withers. Open the inside heel. Yeah, and straight. Open the inside knee and toe to the inside: ask for shoulder in. Yes. Now straight. Relax in the walk and let him just move in the open relaxation of his body. There you go. Good.

Good, look at me, open your inside heel, lift his inside shoulder, outside leg back a little bit, lift both hands a little bit. There, yeah-yeah. There you go. You just did your half-pass. Good work. That was beautiful. That was beautiful. Good job.

18]

That's what I was trying to say last time: your need for a recipe that you want to explore and not knowing if you're going through the process, pedagogically, in the correct way. That's how he's using your energy for him to resist against you.

"I don't know what I'm doing, and I'm doing this, and I'm not sure if it's working…" He's like, "She don't know what the hell she's doing." And he's using that to stay far away from you, because there's no way for him to trust the quality of your question. If we want him to pay attention we have to teach him how to pay attention. We have to give him all of the chances possible he can have to win.

What I think is really important is to first identify the things that you need to feel safe enough to ask him a question and trust that he hears you. When you can do that, you've found the space of silence inside yourself. Work out of that space and don't leave. That's the only space from which horses can hear us. Horses speak in whispery voices. If they go any louder than that, we're pushing too hard.

If I ask you to do something that doesn't make sense, don't

do it. This is not that kind of lesson. We only get as far as we feel safe enough to understand, and that's as far as we need to go, okay? Why the tears?

This is what I'll say: life is each of our story and each of our story is life. All relationships are a life full of stories. A story full of life. Us. If our love for our horses is a feather in the hat, our understanding of our horses is wings on the wind. That's what being with horses is all about. Learning how to be with horses better.

There are days when my pony and I will just sit in the arena for an hour. I'll pull out the pedestal, sit in a chair, and take a book, (because he really loves to be read to), and I'll read to him. As he feels fit, he will stand up on the pedestal, stretch his body out, get down and just relax. He'll do that for a whole hour. And then, when he's ready, he'll turn towards the door, and I know he wants to go for his walk around the farm. The way we invite horses to answer our questions influences the answers they offer.

So much of our relationship with our horses is built on our need to hold all of the power. Such pedagogy keeps us deaf and blind to the beauty and the help horses have to offer us, not just in working with them, but in being better people becoming human as well as in understanding. Generally, in the horse world, there's not a lot of, *I make mistakes and I'm thankful that people still appreciate what I do.* We don't often give horses that same grace.

The brilliance of epiphanies is that you see the way you wish you would have been. This is the pain of learning. It's also the joy of learning. There needs to be room for taking time, feeling what you feel, and feeling it. Learn from this space. And knowingness, the certainty to know, can only come from surrender and acceptance. You can't make yourself do this. You have to walk into it with open hands and an equally open heart. Your mind is gonna try to run off and protect what was and what feels safe. What is familiar. When your mind is nuts, your body is tight and your breath is halfway.

When my mind takes control of the situation, I need to find my breath. I just need to find my breath. And I need to allow myself to go back to the safest space I have ever felt in my life and just rest there in the moment for a moment. Your horse understands this. You become this for your horse. And that's how being with horses in epic peacefulness begins to blossom.

Horses are magnificent creatures. They have so much to teach us about growing in a healthy way, outside of expectation, in which everything they can achieve with us is achievable if we allow it. If we open ourselves up to the journey, they will show us every step of the way. They will show us how to ask the questions for the answers we need. You're finding that space, I can feel. You're not so heavy this time. Good work. Let me see what you've been working on.

19]

1)
Like today, in his warm-up, he's doing what it took all lesson to achieve last week, and each time he's getting close and closer to the door. I think what I really love, is that he comes here every week and is less afraid than the week before.

2)
I'm learning that horses are the people whose lives they're in; like politics flowing downstream from money. It is usually either a promised dream happening or a dreamlike horizon receding too fast for you to catch.

That said, we get trust from time. We get help from trust. We get safety from help. For me, this is the definition of a healthy, healing relationship with the soul-wounded ones who are teaching me how to love them just because I do, beyond the swapping out pawn shop transactional zig for zag.

For him it seems, up until now, safety under a rider has been as elusive as a rail bird. But now that he's found it, it's really cool to see his mind begin to bloom into a world where he feels possible being with people in this way. His body was in bad shape as long as he felt like he had to protect his head from our hands. Once he started feeling safer, his whole way of moving changed. It's like he's being introduced to himself for the first time. He's the new world he's discovering.

3)

I think the magic of horses, though, is that they let you know when they want to do better and aren't afraid of miracles, you know? Sometimes, they'll show you how to make it happen. They'll guide the way.

4)

I'm convinced that horses communicate with people in the best way that people can hear horses. Sometimes, a horse's voice can arrive at people in many different ways.

It was like with him, when you said, "Hey,".... I mean, I didn't invite you to bring him down earlier because I wasn't sure he wanted to. But, when you said, "Hey, the bodyworker said we just need to find a way to loosen his back." That was the first time you'd ever said that, and for me, that was an omen from him saying, "Nahshon, here's the answer that we need your help finding."

So, remember, we took him to the hill in back of the indoor arena and let him graze while he was standing on the incline to create some space, and on the way back inside, I told you how he'd just said, "I'm ready for you to ride." (You see how he's licking and chewing as we talk about this?)

5)

If I feel tension in my body and I breathe into it, I usually will see a picture in my head, and it tells me where to go and what to do next:

19)

For me, hearing horses has more to do with my own self-awareness than it does with trying to find the horse's voice.

Maybe the simple truth of it all, this participation in partnership practice of horse-humans being is so hard to believe because it seems counter-intuitive to what is believed to be true.

I believe in horses and humans in partnership. How that partnership is created is up to the partnership itself.

The partnership is where the magic happens. The magic is a black swan of unknowing; where fear is an unfolding, lifelong lesson about everything that left couldn't stay. How everything that stayed couldn't leave, and how every miracle is a reflection of life. The time that's left isn't as long of a journey as you'd like it to be.

That said, I must admit that this work often leaves my curiosity feeling like a failure wanting to do more good.

6)
I think it's important for people not to ask their horse's questions that aren't so big that they don't understand the answers they're receiving. Just a tiny next step is enough.

You have to keep the rungs of that ladder close enough so that it's not too far to reach the next step. When the rungs of the ladder are too far away, we're stuck with steps too big, going nowhere, instead of taking small steps to get where we'd like to go.

7)
Time. Trust. Safety. Help: Relationship is how the horses know that you won't ask them to do more than they can do, thus allowing the space for them to relax into your question.

For me, it's maybe easier to find the answer because it's not my answer to find. Rather, it's the horse's to give.

Healthy relationships mean maturity and patience.

8)
It takes a lot of courage to see horses as they are, not just the purpose we want them to serve.

9)
It's hard to find joy in the process when you can't find contentment in their answer to your question, which is always the next step.

10)
There's a lot of value in enough. But, what is it? Where do we get it? How do we know when we've found it?

20]

And so the horse comes in. He's out of his mind. He's scared. He has all of this jewelry in his mouth for which neither his mind nor his body has been properly prepared. His back is tight, inverted, and his hind legs are stuck out behind his body. And he's angry…very angry.

So I rode him around. We put a snaffle on him that gave him some tongue relief… and that was the thing about his double bridle: the snaffle was a KK, and his Weymouth was a Mullen Mouth; it's just a straight bar across the tongue. So, there's maximum pressure on this horse's tongue.

I told his person that I would much rather try and figure out the cause of the problem instead of focusing on the symptom. Otherwise, I can't help. So anyway, I kept the horse with me for two lessons: I rode him during his lesson, in which he was frustrated and just needed to move, and so I let him, and then I kept him for another lesson, and I rode him while I was teaching the next person.

In the beginning, he was in a double bridle. By the end, I was riding him around with just a string around his neck. I stopped him, and he kept throwing his head and flinging both of his reins to one side of his neck. So, I took the reins off. And he licked, and chewed, and lowered his head.

Then he looked back at me with asking eyes, and I was like, "Really?" So, I took his bridle off, and he totally let down. The problem was that he'd become quite burned out on the bit and bridle rein. So now we know where to start. The other horse in the arena helped too.

And at that moment, the horse was safer with a string around his neck than a double bridle in his mouth. His lesson turned into a meditation for me on what it really cost the horse for us to sit on them and feel like we're in control.

When we can get beyond thought, there's a space of love. If we can be safe inside that space with horses, then horses will have that frame of reference with us as home. Home is safe. And when we're with them, we're not looking for a place to be because we're in our bodies from which the quality of our questions are rooted. That place beyond thought where love lives. That's what horses understand, first.

Then it turns into a really, really beautiful ritual where you know what makes the work special, regardless of what the work is, is the ability for the horse to relax into the feeling of safety of that space in you beyond thought.

So much of so many horses' lives with people is built around a pretext, which ruins some, and almost ruins many more.

20)

And so, if we can stay beyond that space in our practice of being with horses, then we allow ourselves to be available enough for horses to explore what not having to protect themselves from our questions feels like. The work (which is more powerful in small doses, like eating flowers for medicine), is what our greed does.

21]

It's taken my young horse five years to not have anxiety attacks when I put the saddle on his back. I was ready to retire him. He's only eight. He came to me like that. He'll be nine this year. I was brushing him in the wash bay and I only pull him out when he's at his stall door and says he wants to hang out with me. Otherwise, I just leave him alone because he's sound, and he has Nova to play with. They have plenty of room to play hard and keep each other in really good shape.

I love on him when I'm cleaning his stall, or he and Nova's paddock, if he wants me to, and they gallop around and keep each other in good shape. But Monday…? Tuesday….? What is today, Wednesday? Yeah, Monday, he was at his stall door and looked at me and said, "I want to hang out with you."

And so I brushed him, and I just felt this really soft, warm tingling feeling in my body, and I said, "You're ready to put the saddle on?" And he took a big, deep breath in and blew it out, so I put the saddle pad on, and there was no problem. I was like, "This is cool. Are you sure you're ready for the saddle?" He took another deep breath. I put the saddle on, and the girth, which usually would make him explode...

For a long time, in the year-and-a-half I was riding him, he was just frantic. I stopped, and we just did in-hand work and work from the ground to rehab him. But still, internally, he was a volcano waiting to erupt. The anxiety didn't go away. And so, once the vet said he was all sound in his body and movement, I stopped working with him and told him to let me know when he's ready to start back up.

So, since December, we've been averaging a lesson a month. And only when he was at his door and said he was ready to come out. It was always at the end of the day when I was done with my chores.

And so, I put the saddle on, and I had him ground tied in the wash bay. My mom came down and was talking to her cats, Beauty and Ginger Bacon, and he was really fascinated by that. But then he just started lickin'-and-chewin', lickin'-and-chewin', and he's never done that…ever.

He'd been seen by the vet, and the shoer had gotten his feet right because when we started, his feet were a negative ten, and now his left one is at a seven, and his right one is at a nine. I just couldn't find any farriers who cared to help me get him healthy, and I get it: he's huge, volatile, and was absolutely horrible to shoe. I totally understand. He was dangerous because he was scared.

None of the advice I'd sought out from other trainers, or methods, or what I read in books helped. The vet suggested

I sedate him, but he'd just metabolize through it. It wouldn't even touch him. Then, like I said, he met this gifted young shoer at the barn I was boarding at before we bought this place, and the two of them just fell in love. And so I asked the kid if he'd hire us as clients. We've all worked together happily ever after, for three years now.

Anyway, after he was all saddled and girthed up, I sat directly across the aisle from where he was standing in the wash bay after I felt more certain that he wouldn't blow up, and just watched him process: he had these beautiful fluttering butterfly wing blinks, and then he started yawning…yawning…yawning. Then he just stood there with his eyes closed. At that moment, I felt like that was my greatest accomplishment for him, as his person, up to that point: we've waded through the memories enough.

I'm happy because now I think I don't have to buy another horse for riding. Either way he's safe with me: he has a home forever. But, I would much rather it be him, because I love him, and I know that I'm his person, and he knows that he is my horse…

22]

I think this is where you can help me as a teacher, a trainer, and a sharer of ideas about horses. Where (and I'm gonna be brave here) are the strong places that you see in my process and the things that aren't so strong that need to get better?

I'm trying to be courageous enough to not assume that everybody sees the education of horses and their people like I do. What I'm asking, from a pedagogic point of view, is if I was supportive of you, in the ways that you needed me to be supportive, to make the progress that you made possible?

No, I don't get frustrated having to repeat something over to you. Because the fact of the matter is that you hear what I'm asking you to do when you hear it. Also, each of our training sessions together only lasts an hour. And, in all fairness, you're still trying to feel out my way of teaching enough to trust it, and I understand that. I understand, too, that mine is a very different approach.

For me as a teacher, I also have to feel safe enough to not be impatient with the people learning from me. If I'm teaching from a place where you and your horse's well-being is my only goal, you'll eventually get what I'm asking you to do.

And we'll celebrate you and your horse's time with me with every step we take along the road of understanding.

Teaching in this way is really helpful for me because it will take as long as it takes for you to relax enough to try and understand the language I'm asking you to embody for your horse the first time. But, it usually doesn't take as long the second time. For me, that's wonderful progress.

What I see working with you, though, is your attachment to expectations that you assume I have of you that I just don't have. You working through that anxiety is a very difficult treasure hunt for precious facts of the matter about your love for your horses and wanting to be the best you can for them. But expectations and assumptions can sometimes be very heavy trouble from the past for students of the horse to carry. Empathy is insight into another's acts of being. Being present is the guide.

That said, I think it's fantastic when your horse is moving healthier this time around than he was moving last time around. That's a huge improvement because it lets me know I'm being clear enough for you to feel what I'm asking you to feel.

I can only give what is mine to give. I try to keep the help I have to offer flowering from as pure a place as possible, so I can hear where you're coming from enough to start out of the space we're in together. Teaching is a belief in life.

22)

Remi, my young kill pen rescue, is able to canter next to me, in-hand, while I'm walking on the ground next to him. Being as big as he is, and me not being as big as I am, this is an example of how the conversation between us is more important than either of us individually. This is the rules blossoming from the relationship so that there's reciprocity. But, his body bears the scars of someone in his previous world trying to make a relationship out of rules that resulted in resistance. We're all a little lost sometimes.

We meet all of this stuff in the beginning, and then we come to a place where we trust each other, and then the work can be possible. My job is to follow you wherever I need to to get you where you want to go if I can. As a teacher, this is a really important space for me to hold for people so that more people and their horses don't get left out anymore. Time is the miracle. Waiting is the magic. Patience is the key.

23]

I think that the fact that you've relaxed in your body enough to find the answer feelingly is absolutely magnificent. I mean, really! You meditated on what you needed to be and shape-shifted into that. You were calm because you meditated on calm and that's what you became for your horse. Because of that, he felt calm enough to ask you, "when?" And you felt calm enough to tell him "not yet." And the lines of communication stayed open.

Horses live out of an inner space where everybody is just what they are, and everybody is allowed to just be that. Everything blossoms out of that; everything blossoms out of their experience of the world feelingly. Which, for me just means knowing how to listen. This is what it's like to be a teacher.

For me, whether it's training horses or healing horses, if you follow them, they'll lead you and they'll grow you. But people can't find that space until they've gotten past their addiction to happiness, meaning the use of horses despite the negative consequences.

What good is it hiding from yourself, right? If you can't be who you are, doing what you're doing, then why are you doing it? If you're not who you are while you're doing this,

23)

then what you're doing really isn't real because there are no rules. There are no healthy boundaries. Healthy boundaries make horses feel safe. Healthy boundaries help people feel safe, too.

Do you trust yourself enough to hear what your horse is saying and know what you have to say is worth them listening to? Horses being silently loud, powerful, challenging, smart, sensitive, and miraculous is the truest thing that ever was. Why are you afraid of that? What is the reason that you would try to hide that part of yourself that your horse is trying to bloom you into?

For my horses, our work together is always around the question of why we're looking back if we're going forward. What is the value in looking back? Who's there? Who do you wish was there? And why isn't right now enough for you? What do you want right now to be?

So you have a horse who was pulled from the wild. You've given him a safe space for him to understand and trust that the past is the past. This is where the both of you inner-are together in the space that you've created for him to be safe enough for him to be safe enough with you. How were you able to do that for him but not yourself?

And how, when you stopped putting the onus in someone else's hands, you found the answer in your own. Isn't that the mercy? Some horses become problems for their people when their people believe they need someone else to save them from themselves.

Personally, a world is being built around me by being safe in a horse's heart. They're teaching me that there's no difference between me being inside of their hearts and everything I am becoming in the world.

When I got Nova, he said, "If you take care of me, I'll take care of you." He came to me in a dream and said, "You're my person."

"How is this gonna work?" I asked.

He said, "You'll take care of me and I'll take care of you."

I did not understand that this horse had found all of the shattered pieces to me that I had lost and put them in their correct place. He taught me not to run from myself, and that if I trust that being where I am is enough, I can be everything I need to be for the space I'm in. You don't have to know if you trust it.

Every fear that I've had that he's walked me through was my next step on my journey into myself. Because of that, I'm talking to you. I'm so thankful for how these situations don't make sense until you're past trying to understand what they mean.

23)

When you trust each step you take, you can see everything there is to see. But, you must trust each step, and you must trust yourself enough to trust each step. And you, then, begin to understand that each step is its own light showing the space where you are in the world at that moment.

It's not your horse you're afraid of: It's not his power, it's yours. It's your power. And it's not your power to do what you're able to do. It's your power to be all that you are. That's all he sees. And all you have to do, my dear, is find the courage to accept it.

I never thought that my life could be built out of helping horses heal. And I never thought that there were so many other people who could hear horses. And I never thought so many people would ever feel like they needed permission to listen to what their horses were telling them.

Who is it that you see in yourself that you're afraid of accepting? If you were to trust your gut, who do you see? If we could make the future, the past, and the present coalesce into a single, beautiful moment, who would be there? We have the person who feels like someone needs to save them. We have the person who's learning to save themselves. But that person who felt like they needed someone to save them grew into the person who made a choice not allowing someone else to decide to save them. Who does that person grow into, just because that's where you're horse is leading you?

What's the reason you're afraid of transcending? Why are you afraid of letting go of what doesn't grow you anymore? What's the reason for not becoming more of who you are right now; valuable? Because that's what you're afraid of; you're afraid of the growth.

It sounds like you've already found some good peace in your world. You're not speaking from a place of angst. You're speaking from a place of, "I've done the work and I've created a space for myself that feels safe, and now I the choice to feel safe enough to decide if I want to grow out of the space that I've made for myself to feel safe enough inside of."

Do you want to plant that flower in your garden and watch it grow? I can tell you this though: if you decide to take this next step, it's for other people… to know that you're just a drop in the ocean, and the ocean is there because you're a drop in it. So, what do you want for yourself so that you can help? When you come into that space of service, the whole world becomes holy. You'll begin to understand the power and the magic that your hands hold because you're not afraid of sharing love.

When you share love, that's what you become, and everything you do will bloom out of that. If your home is your heart, you always find what you seek. And the world has to be crazy for people who have the courage to be love to love in it. Maybe that's the whole purpose of it all.

I know you've touched heaven because you know how to follow horses. Now, the question is, do you have the courage to share it? That's where your horse is calling you to. This is religionless love without dogma; and servanthood without guilt…or obligation. There are no should-s. It's just a choice. Either way, you're okay. There's just the possibility of regret.

So, it all comes down to the comfort of where your heart is. Are you willing to let it keep growing? Are you willing to stop being that little one who is waiting for someone to save them? Is what lies ahead worth laying her down? Because all your fear is stemming from that—and forgiving whoever taught you how to be that way. Letting it die so you can keep living and learn how to be.

This has nothing to do with what you're doing, and it has everything to do with who you are doing what you do. There's nothing to be afraid of when you are who you are. Now, isn't that some shit?

It's the way forward, and if you decide to do it, your horse will make so much more sense to you. You won't be feeling like he's expecting you to be more for him than you are. It's not about control. You've already opened yourself up to hear your horse. Now the question is, will you listen?

Your horse wants you to be. Stop acting like you're being by doing all this other stuff, like in a drag show. Letting go is a ladder whose every rung is a universe full of flame glow, lighting the way to see beyond the benefits of illusion. A lot of training methods have grown out of that space: horses are ruined because people are hiding. Horses are blamed for human ignorance... and then this cycle of suffering continues because everybody feels like they have to play the role. What are the values of allowing the fire to continue to burn? What is the disappearing? Hoping someone sees you so they will save you? It's like The Waiting Place in Dr. Suess's *Oh, The Places You Will Go*. Your horse is wondering why you're continuing to wait. Everybody's worthy of being free, but not everyone feels like they deserve to be free. Our freedom doesn't happen without our permission.

Some horses are not from this world. To have one is the privilege and the gift of a lifetime. They are wise enough to know that they can only help us to the extent that we're willing to be helped. Those who believe are healed.

24]

For me, there is no beauty without the broken. The broken are the only ones I go for broke for. When perfection is no longer an option, then we truly are alive: to move forward, something must be lost to be gained. That's the whole purpose of this thingamajig called life, I think. And the eyes that we look out into the world with determine the world we see.

We either accept that the ocean is the ocean, or we waste our time trying to mop up the ocean off the beach. And we only waste our time trying to mop the ocean off the beach if we don't see that the ocean is the ocean and that the beach comes from the ocean. The beach is also the ocean. The beach is not the beach. The beach is the ocean.

I think in the holiness of each moment it's really important to understand that each moment is another chance to learn how to know by continuing to walk and learn and grow. That each moment is possible. That's what makes it a sacred thing: possibility. It is whatever it is. It is holy. Holy is help.

Everything is holy. It is holy. Not because we try to make it holy, but because we accept it for what it is. When we try to make it holy, we cannot see that flowers were stars shining on the underside of roots. There's light down here, too, but only when your eyes find their balance again.

And this is what my work with the wounded-soul ones, especially my little grey Yoda-pony, has taught me about equids: they understand more about us than we're capable of allowing them to communicate. This is why when we're afraid of them, it's because there's so much for us to learn.

The other day I read that if the four and a half billion years of Earth's geological age were reduced down into a 12-hour window, humans would only be ten seconds old. If we were to translate Earth's four and a half thousand million birthdays into a single year, an average human life expectancy would be one and a quarter seconds. Losing something to gain something is still the same story that's been told since the story began. Every body is here. Every mind, the hereafter.

And maybe the purpose of this journey is to learn to see ourselves more. My love for my horses is teaching me how to love better. Horses help human beings help people become human beings. Anything that leads you to love is true.

And no matter where you're at, you either see through the eyes of love or not love. And not love is hell. If you see with the eyes of love, everything is heaven, even hell. Because all you see is love. It's very simple, which is why it's so hard. It's not easy because we want it to mean something other than what it means because it really isn't that shiny until it is.

Understanding is a labor pain. It's full of expansion and contraction, like the breath. When you're expanding, you're facing your fear. When you're contracting, you're holding your heart in your hands and watching it beat. The tears. The tears. The tears, you know. That's part of the process. And that's where the non-attachment comes in: in the acceptance of *this is where I'm at right now in this place.* And this place is what it is with me in it, right now. Are there always more places to go? Yeah, there are. And that's the value of a moment: it teaches you that forever is not so long.

It always is, like the soul. It's always there. And no matter where it is, there it is. And where you are stops being special when you realize that if you're not there, you're somewhere else and then you're there. And you're there for the purpose that you need to be there for. And when you are there and not attached to it, you begin to see that there is just another there no matter where there is, and there you are because that's where you're supposed to be. And when you offer help, you find your next step.

25]

1)
The Horse: *Let yourself go.*
Me: I can't.
The Horse: *You gotta do it.*

2)
The most valuable thing someone can offer, I think, is an open heart. Everybody being welcome is truth beyond belief when we become less of only ourselves and more of all that is. Whoever shall come, may.

3)
My gift-horse Remi is like a hundred-and-twenty-watt light bulb in a thirty-watt lamp. Sometimes, he makes me feel like he's an alien that took a wrong turn and accidentally walked onto the earth from a portal where the mountains meet the sea—where my questions aren't a place of peace-appliquéd comfort that is safe enough for him to be vulnerably generous with me.

His sometimes over-complicating sensitivities show me how taking care of my blessings is heaven. It's like being led to a place you aren't sure where. All you know is that each step along the way is too beautiful an offering not to receive. Now, because of him, my only expectation of horses is for them to feel free enough to let me know who they are when they're ready and what they need from me so that they can exist outside of their trauma, again, if they want to.

4)
Remi's teaching me how to not be afraid of holding that space of infinite love and zero control that my self-acceptance of others is. That said, I think a lot of our problems with our horses originate from us not really knowing what we want and then making a mess we can't clean up trying to get it. Like spending so much money on horses trying to fix them, and then putting them back into the same training program that broke them down in the first place.

5)
And how the horses so few people want are the horses that have the answers almost everyone needs. But still, I'm grateful that my hands love the process of thinking through their bodies, using what I know, listening to them, and allowing myself not to know so that I can truly try to hear what they're saying to me.

6)
Even more than release from pressure, horses seek peace.

7)
Joy is something only heartbreak can bring. Happiness hopes

heartbreak won't come, but joy comes from heartbreak. And you realize that in the heartbreak, it only stays dark when you're afraid of the dark. When you stop being afraid, everything is gleaming, glowing, bright, shining light, like the moon.

8)
The majority of the horses I work with are pretty hopeless cases when you hope for happiness. But, when you live for joy and let their pain break your heart so that joy can bloom… there are no flowers without the shit. And then the sun starts to shine, and here they are, in the perfection of all they can be, and then they relax. There's not this tension that I'm working out of what I think they should be. I accept them for who they are and allow them to grow regardless of how they arrived.

9)
Stillness and time are how answers to questions come, which is what listening is. And when the answer is "no, thank you," I honor that.

10)
But, this is how I know: when I feel like I'm banging my head against the wall, and nothing is changing, it's time for them to go. That's it. It doesn't matter how I feel about it.

It's hard. It's a hard practice, but it's valuable: I'm offering, and you say "no," and that's okay.

25)

Otherwise, they're working against themselves, and your causing more pain. And if part of the practice is to help ease the suffering; and if they say "no" and you don't respect it, then you're causing suffering, and that's really bad karma. That comes back hard.

I know that, and I understand that sometimes you have to come back down to the earth and play by the rules of the earth:

If we move beyond the empire of ideas and categorization, where enlightenment is the opposite of ignorance and surrender is all there is...

26]

1)
This is what I've learned about working with traumatized horses: that they're so survival-based that they sometimes go into a training session wondering, "Am I going to live through this?" And how so many people don't have any framework to understand that true interconnectedness is respect for difference. With trauma, the room is always bigger than the door. Anything can be real or true.

2)
For me, the beginning of a relationship with the ones in need of healing from humans happens when I accept their ability to choose freely whether or not they're willing to lead me through repairing pottery with silver or gold lacquer. Like the process of mending wounds we've inflicted using our desire for connection as code for a need to control.

3)
The art of helping hurt horses is not freedom on parole camouflaged in friendship. The art of helping horses heal is total availability creating safe space for the honest sharing of their experiences to fill. This work takes the time it takes, and that's all the time we need. Time is the ocean. Teardrops are salt water. Every journey is a circle. Life.

4)

With horses, when you can move beyond what you've learned to be afraid of, and it still feels right, even if it doesn't make sense, that's love. You just want them to be happy. That said, sometimes you have every good thing to offer, and they still say "no." If you honor their answer, that's love.

5)

And if understanding is beyond the light and the dark of the world as it is, then surrender is beyond understanding. In the past, before I knew how to sit with my own pain, explore it, heal it, and love it enough to learn to use my body to help them be better in *their* bodies, I have unintentionally hurt horses.

I didn't know I was afraid of myself, so I ran from my shadow, which was so scary and tall because my back was to the light. But, I got tired of running. Running is exhausting. So, I stopped to try and catch my breath, and in the pause between inhales and exhales discovered how beautiful the world is, and that time is a gift. The earth too.

6)

I don't want to destroy everything I touch. If these horses are the earth, where on earth is not worthy of my love? Where? If horses are the earth, if this is what I have the opportunity to care for, love, and be thankful for every day; a place for my heart to have joy… and to share joy… and be joy…

7)

To see the cycle of it all, when a horse is so much more through their body, and consequently so much more in their mind because we're over their heart with our heart when we ride them. Having that heart alignment in the seat to feel what the horses are telling us. It's learning to trust yourself enough to trust the horse enough to teach you how to trust yourself, like rune stones or the guardian angels that gut feelings are.

8)

Was deciding not to run anymore hard? As hard as Remi accepting relaxation or Mohawk opening up her heart enough to not kill me when she could have. But, if I didn't work to change to be better for my horses, how could I ask my horses to be better for me?

And to what end? That horses aren't a means to an end. But instead, are allowed to be an end in and of themselves. My ambition is to let them have a voice that's heard and that they can trust so that they can understand that they don't have to be afraid of not understanding or asking questions. That's the end: to end as much suffering as I can. Horses are holy things for me. Heart first, always.

27]

Now we see that when the space is open for him to be okay being afraid, and I'm not trying to not make him afraid, I just want to make him feel welcome, then he calms down. And so that was the problem, it seems. It wasn't that he was afraid. It was that he didn't feel welcomed enough to not be. He would spook at something because he had never felt protected by people, and then he was judged as a spooky horse. When what he was really saying is, *"I really don't understand what this means, and if you just give me a little time…just give me a little time. Just give me five minutes to stand here and look. Don't push me through it. Don't click. Don't cluck. Just stand here with me so that I can see it. I'm really not stupid. I just need to know that your question is as safe as it can be before I try to answer it out of that non-guarded inner space where I'm still all mine."*

And because the body and the brain work in concert with each other, when your horse arrived with a mind that hadn't been at peace with people around in at least five years, all he needed was to be offered space to be okay. So, with my hands, my heart, and my mind, and my energy, I told him, "You are welcome here, in this space, as long as you're willing to try not to always live like everything people do is dangerous, and likely to cause pain, or be a threat, even though that's been almost your whole experience up to now. Also, can I help you not feel so unsettled by offering you a treat?"

With understanding, we can usually get as far as we can go, and the journey for me with broken horses is this: healed horses help heal hurting people. Healed people help heal hurting worlds by not being afraid of listening from the one you're listening to's point of view enough to feel what they are feeling. Trust happens when fear turns into curiosity.

So, if you believe your horse is the way he is because of you, then I'm interested in learning the reason you are the way you are with your horse. And this is what I hear you saying when you are over-explaining to try and defend yourself against the criticism you've assumed I'm storing up like ammo for a coup d'etat on your confidence in your abilities as a horse person, or the lack thereof. Please correct me if I'm not on the right track, okay? Here it goes:

> I have for so long squashed my anger down and squashed it down again, only to be called nice or to be silenced and/or taken advantage of. I think it is more than overdue that I reset the scale so that I can carefully drive forward with my words and, yes, my intentions, too, with grace and knowledge of the rules of the road. The reason I'm here is to ask for your help to create and carry forward a heart-centered mindset of growth in mind for me and my horse, and no longer at the detriment of myself.

27)

That said, life wasn't working for this horse before he came to you, and that's not your fault. If you'd asked me before you got him, though, I wouldn't have thought him to be the best first, second, or even third choice for you, in my professional opinion. But, this is where we're at. I'll do the best I can to help if you'd still like me to try, and not at the expense of neither you, me, or your horse, because he's my friend. I've witnessed some really beautiful partnerships blossom out of the bottom of the bucket. Sometimes, that's actually the best place to start.

I see the potential in this horse and your ability to make an honest effort when you're not afraid of being judged for not having all the tools you need to ask the questions to get the answers you're asking for. Even more still, what I greatly admired and appreciated in our lesson yesterday was you understand the limit you could go and when to say to me, "Okay, I need your help again."

If I'm an effective teacher, I have to allow myself to let my students teach me how to teach them. And this is what I've learned so far: when people feel safe enough to feel vulnerable, they always try the very best they can. In being yourself, nobody has to lose except the person you're not being true to, which is the miracle.

28]

Part of me feels like no one can ever really "arrive," but part of me also wants to get "there," wherever there is. But maybe the answer is you can always only get closer to something, like a line that continually approaches a given curve but does not meet it at any finite distance.

We all have to walk our own road of understanding. Each step in the right direction is our eyes seeing that the mean words, the mean actions, and the mean thoughts that we inflict on horses and humans are products of un-forgiven unkindnesses inflicted on us. Unhealed heart hurt is a disease that's only cured when it's no longer nice to be mean anymore.
We've spent far too much life being purveyors of pain for horses and each other.

The wisdom of pain without the understanding of pain is a riddle: we are not our pain. If you don't understand the intention from which a request has arisen, then the request can sound like somebody speaking to you in tongues. That said, we are all from where we are from. But, the only thing that matters, right here and now, it that this is where we are right here and now.

Here and now is where my next step forward is always found. Which, with regards to the rehabilitative aspect of me helping horses, is in love; creating healing out of hurt by conjuring salve from suffering for hearts in need of being soothed enough to feel alright again; or eyes to see with for those in need of a safe sight; or power in need of a mind mature enough to choose its battles carefully by considering the emotional consequences of punishment instead of being brave enough to ask horses questions. To hear what they have to tell us.

And this is what I've learned so far about working with horses with major trauma: you can't help them be better by making them feel worse. Punishment is not a very useful chisel to sculpt healthy horses out of. Punishment is anger. Anger is the protector of pain, which kills the curiosity that conscious listening encourages by having an attachment to outcomes, which is nothing more than an addiction to superiority: "Just ride her through it" or "She's not learning anything if you're not on her back" or "She's just being a mare, make her mind." These are not stepping stones on the path to partnership with our horses. Partnership with our horses is the path.

I used to think that when my horses were naughty, they were purposely trying to provoke a fight, but they weren't. I didn't know they were trying to tell me something was not right, that they were really worried about what was upsetting them so much, and that I had to figure it out to fix it. Conscious listening is what allows us to not take ourselves so seriously and still have healthy boundaries. Healthy boundaries teach us how to search for the right questions and slowly build our horse's trust in us enough to try to answer.

When I ask a horse a question and am waiting for an answer, I try not to think about what I'm going to ask him or her next. This is one of the ways I practice trusting myself enough to calm my insecurities, just breathe and consciously listen. For me, the power, the miracles, and the magic of my work with our friends swims in the space between our questions. And sometimes, the answer to our question lies in us learning to ask our questions differently.

Horses are the light I'm learning to see. When I follow them, I'm able to find heaven in every step. And in every step, I'm being taught how not to be afraid of getting to know the person waiting for me on the inside. His damaged places, his weakness, his wishes, all of it, and dealing with everything I can, as much as I can.

I once heard it said, or maybe I read it somewhere, that when you see the light, will you be worthy of yourself enough to respect who you are becoming? That's when life begins. Life is the light horses are teaching me to see. When I follow them, I'm able to find heaven in every step.

28)

I don't know what human being is perfect, but horses are the light I'm learning to see. When I follow them, I'm able to find heaven in every step. And in every step, I'm being taught, more and more. How not to be afraid of how much of a difference it makes for your heart to be in the right place.

29]

And this is what I've learned from my work with traumatized horses so far:

When I have the courage to allow the answer to be more play, more time, and more space for myself to embrace the part of me that's still sometimes scared and confused about being able to see how everybody will find their light when they walk their road,

I find this feeling in my bones that I'm able to use to set my body free with language while listening to life, letting go of the fear of not knowing so that the problem of being afraid, not always meaning danger, can be unraveled as much as possible.

And even though the work is always defined by what the work is, I'm always striving for a blossoming, clearer, more concise communication, which is a mutually health-giving horse-human connection. Also, there are whole brain hemispheres between the journey and the destination. So, strive softly.

30]

I had a horse come here once, Sebastian, who came to me so broken that he didn't want to be better. And so, I sent him home. It was important for me to respect that. That's still a bitter pill to swallow.

It can take a very long time for a horse to trust me enough to entertain my questions enough to feel safe enough to answer the questions I asked them to answer, and allow myself the courage to accept whatever answer they give me—which can sometimes be very painful. Things don't always turn out the way I want them to. From that, I am learning that when I go in with a certain expectation, then we're not giving the horse a fair shot at opening up and telling us the truth.

And so my question to you is, where's the doubt? Because it sounds like you're trying to control something that doesn't need to be controlled. There are different levels of communication with horses, for sure, but when we just allow ourselves to let it flow, it's always there, like love… Or a tennis ball in a tennis match, when it arrives, let it. But be prepared to let it go, like the breath—when you allow it the space and time to do what it needs to do, it always does. So it also is with listening.

I've found that when I don't feel like I need to control, I'm able to hear more because horses feel safe and listen enough to initiate questions. And there's this whole universe in waiting between the question and the answer where the process of the direction of the conversation goes.

We want to communicate with our horses, but what is the space within ourselves that we're cultivating to communicate with them? Is our process an invitation for them to enter with us, or are we going to demand that they talk to us?

The room is always bigger than the door, but is the door open? If it is, is it equal access? Then you come to this point where you don't see the need for the door anymore, and then you don't see the need for a room anymore, and then all there is the space to be shared. Then horses can also ask you where you're hurting or how they can help your heart heal. They do all of the time, and part of that offering is them helping us understand that we can't help outside of the space we've been helped, and so they show us how.

In helping horses, I've realized that they don't get better until I realize what they need me to realize about myself so I can hear them. Then the answers come. Conversation is a mutual attempt, like a healthy relationship. No one dominates. Trusting yourself enough to feel like you don't need to control the space between questions and answers is the lesson. We lose so much power by feeling like we need to own it, but it's not ours. It's everyone's. That's why it's so powerfully useful.

You obviously have it. You obviously understand the common thread of being in all manifestation and you're trying to own it. And you can't because it's already yours. You're trying too hard. So much so that you can't relax into your try. Feel your feet on the floor. Take a deep breath, ask the question, and wait, and observe everything that pops up while you're waiting: the anxieties about yourself, the judgements around the anxieties about yourself... those are all the things trying to push you into the impatient ownership of it. Then you're trying to model yourself after the image of the method-maker, which you're not. You're already everything that you need to do this. You just have to trust yourself enough to experience the process that allowing your horses to lead you is. They'll show you, but only what they know you're ready for... what they feel safe with you not trying to control them with. That's the path and the journey.

Do we truly want to hear horses if they give us answers we don't want? If not, we're working out of the insecurity of a control technique wearing a communication mask that we need validation. That's not fair. That's not a real question. You see, that's force. Change changes everything.

So I would challenge you to not be too deep. Just trust the depth you're in, and as you relax, the feeling will carry you.

If you try to force it, you will sink. You trust it, and it carries you. Then you're helpful because it's not for you. It's not for you. It's for whoever needs you.

31]

What meets the eye is the last thing. Most people think it's the first thing. But, what meets the eye is the last thing, for sure.

That said, I don't like to make a practice foreseeing the future too often. Instead, I just try to work with what is. I don't really like to infer or speculate because I know enough to know what I don't know, and there is still a lot that I don't know. But, I know that sometimes the lesson is in accepting that a horse is outside of my expectation of what I think he or she should be and that being enough.

For example: I have a horse, my young horse Remi, who is seven, who had really horrible trauma done to one of his ligaments in his back. He's rideable, and I want to ride him, but he doesn't want to be ridden, so I'm not going to. He's cured. His body is good. But mentally, he's not, and he may never be, and what do I do with that except understand that being healed can sometimes be very different than being cured.

So, the first part of it is just being open to whatever the answer may be outside of our desire of what we think it should be. The should is the expectation, and if we're going in with an expectation, then we're really not seeing with eyes that want to see what is to be seen.

And I hear what you're saying, and I agree. I do know how to stay in that space. I live out of that space, and this is how: when I'm afraid and doubts and negativity try to make me run away and hide from the world, I breathe as deeply as I'm able into my love for this life to be full of awareness and surrender so that I may have a clear enough mind to be present, a courageous enough heart to be vulnerable, and a simple enough faith to listen on purpose so that horses may continue to be my help along the way.

To keep it, you have to have the strength not to hold it and allow it to come when you need it. If you're always wanting what you had, you don't get what you need. And each situation is so incredibly different because every horse guides each of us in so many different ways.

Learning to trust this process is difficult. Most people want it so bad that they miss it. That's where a lot of people have a lot of trouble: they want it so bad that they try too hard instead of realizing that all they have to do is accept it. Help from horses isn't something you go and get. It's something you accept, and is only as real as you believe it to be.

32]

Movement is a revelation, you know. If we go back to the idea of undoing what's been done to get you back to where you were before you started, being the definition of a question and forgiveness: we are undoing what's been done to get you back to where you were before you started.

And how this is embodied in the work that I'm trying to do with horses and how the horses that work with me on a regular basis feel safe enough to say: One) I've done a really good job. Two) I'm trying my best. Three) I don't understand what you mean. Four) Is this what you want? Five) I can't do that.

And how opening that space really allows for everything to just be one thing, which is also a beginning. Because we're able to go back and see what was auto-piloted and weave it into a tapestry of different movements: Leg-yield, halt, rein-back. Haunches-in, quarter pirouette. And really helping him understand…

And when you get horses to the place where they're not afraid to talk to you about what went wrong and they tell you how to fix it…

And it's hard to see, but once you see it, it's so clear.

Then meaning goes from just being like just words to a poem. That's what good poetry does to you, and it doesn't make sense until you get to that space. The language of horses is poetry.

But, I think the important part about today is that he's not afraid to be led. He's not second-guessing what I'm asking him to do. He trusts that the answer can be found inside the question.

What's interesting is how much time it's taking him to integrate this information in the halt. Did you see how, when I picked up the reins, he turned around and was like, "Give me a minute."

I can feel him breathing so deeply that his inhales are lifting up the saddle. He used to just breathe just up to his cinch. Now, it's reaching all the way back to his flanks.

33]

I'm learning to put language to things and I am developing a written philosophy to training that doesn't just float around in my head and heart like marine life. So I can share it, I suppose. Here is my training principles polyptych. Thanks for taking the time to read it. Please let me know if it's too foggy. Thanks again.

1)
To be content, we must find joy in the little things and celebrate them deeply and completely. For me, this is a methodical approach to training.

2)
Continuing to learn to be more kind, clear, patient, forgiving, and working hard to allow horses the space to feel special, confident, and heard. For me, these are the intelligent hopes that good judgment is.

3)
A reciprocal feeling of mutual trust, understanding, and an ever-blossoming sense of well-being between horse and human. For me, this is respect.

4)
Follow the horse, and find heaven in every step. For me, this is the journey.

34]

So, my first question to you is: What you can feel in your body?

Okay, I'm going to challenge you to trust your body as much as you can. Your mare and I are going to try and see if we can get you to the place where you can listen to her with your body, with the goal being that your mind quiets down enough to not get stuck behind self-doubt and anger at your body.

This is what I'd like you to do, I want you to try and feel her hind legs in your rib cage. And so, if your tummy's pulled in and your seat bones are going back-and-down and forward-and-up at the same time, your back is too hard. If you bring your shoulder forward, just a bit, to where your ankles are in line with your neck, you seat bones begin to rock from side to side, and the horse's movement becomes like medicine for your spine. Your mind finds stillness when you're able allow your body to follow your mare's movement.

And I can see how you could get really upset at the limits of this body that you're in. That's totally understandable. But, also, I want you to be very cognizant of where the body you're in is trying to meet you, and that it's doing the best that it can.

Now, we're going to use our imagination. Speed your thighs up. Like you're jogging. Quicker! Try not to let your back get too heavy. No lead-back. Now, slower. What I'm seeing the challenge is gonna be, is when I ask you to do something, every excuse that you've ever had is going to show up for why you can't answer my question. Nice transition up into the trot. Good. Now, walk. Speed you thighs up. Bring your shoulders forward a little. More. Now, slow your thighs down. Good. Now, trot.

The biggest thing I've learned during this lesson is how important language is to you. And how the way somebody speaks to you determines whether or not you give yourself permission to try and answer the question I'm asking you to try and answer. Walk.

Now you just proved to everybody, and most importantly yourself, that you could trot. But, when I said "trot" your body shut down because I didn't lead you though the process. So, that lets me know that I need to lead you through the "how."

It's easy for you to be angry at your body for what it can't do when I ask you to trot: You give it a big middle finger: You try. You fail. And because there's no semantic path to help you learn how to know what you are doing, you can't stay calm, and your body braces, and you shut down because you're not sure if you're speaking in a way your mare understands.

Crossing the bridge from not focusing on just being good enough, to becoming complete, or whole, like history truthfully told with the detached clarity of distance listening to what horses hear our human hearts saying about how much more we would know about ourselves if we didn't have to spend so much time un-learning what we've been taught about life as a canyon full of questions no one was taught to ask.

Something is happening that is very important. A door has opened for you to believe in yourself in a way that you couldn't before. And the choice is up to you about whether or not you're going to walk into that door that has just been opened, or if the anger is good enough. Do you see what I'm saying? You have a choice where you haven't had a choice before. See what I mean?

Your life is like: Get on the boat. Your anger is like: I'm afraid of water. Your horse is like: Here's a life vest for your journey to almost healed meaning more than this, if you want.

That's enough for today. You both worked very hard. Thank you. Do you want me to get your wheelchair for you

35]

1)

I think that the really important thing about training horses is that the courage to go slow gets you to your destination a lot faster. I think the challenge that I sometimes run into with horses like him is that some of them need different things from you to help them find the correct answer to the question you're asking them. The most important thing for me is trying to figure out how they learn that my questions are safe to just sit with.

Learning to sit with the question is a big thing with this horse, and what it's teaching him is that I'm not allowed to colonize his body, I'm not allowed to just take his body away from him and do whatever the hell I want with it: and I mean it in the truest sense of that word, like an invasive species of fish taking over a lake: I'm not allowed to be that.

Horses are like people in that way, in that when they feel safe enough in our questions to know that we won't take advantage of them, they have no reason to need to stay afraid. For me, this is the beginning of healing. Truth is like that, I think. This morning, I was talking about the soul's journey with a friend on the phone when she shared how she felt that life was like a movie whose script about what is really happening has already been written." She said, "But, sometimes I go off script, and I get lost in my thoughts, and that's when I suffer."

I thought about what she said inside of a long moment of silence then replied, "That is a beautiful metaphor that I think I'm going to use in an essay I'm writing about learning to trust truth to be itself. And if life is like a movie, and truth is what happens before the movie's beginning and end, and the script is about running our own race, then we suffer when we try to run someone else's… When we use our own personal power to take someone else's personal power away from them." I said, "Thank you for that clarification."

I think that that's the thing with him, and horses like him, and how important it is to know what question you want to ask, and to have a whole bunch of different ways of asking it, if it's an appropriate question, instead of changing the question. Today's question for him is: "Can you be soft?"

> And he's like, "Can you be soft?"
> And I said, "Of course I can be soft?"
> And he said, "Even if I'm hard?"
> And I said, "Well, of course I can."
> And he said, "But, then I can't be hard anymore."
> And I said, "That's exactly right."

With horses, a lot of people know what they want, but they don't know when they've got it. And they don't understand that even if the answer is incomplete, the try is enough when we ask the question from inside of the answer we're looking for. And if we get confusion, and we don't know how to explain the confusion away, do we really understand that question whose answer we're asking for? Because clarity comes from understanding the purpose of a thing. A lifetime in a heartbeat.

I must admit, working with this population of horses got a whole lot easier for me when I started learning how to listen into the gaps and the shadows, where the secrets that kill connection hide instead of staying angry at what I didn't understand. Responsibility feels like blame when we're not prepared to own how our choices negatively impact another. His history is of a horse who's learned to hide from people hiding from themselves behind agendas doing more actual damage than their work.

So there, those two steps were his answer. That was all he could give. If I would have pushed him, I wouldn't have been asking the same question anymore. So, he wouldn't know what answer to give me because the question had changed. And we see that when his try is acknowledged as enough, because we're going in the right direction, he doesn't feel like he has to protect himself and so, in turn, doesn't become resistant.

2)

My niece painted that picture when she was two, in the corner over there. She turned my arena into an art gallery. It was her first commissioned piece of art. And she took a bunch of old crayons, her and my sister, and glued them on onto a piece of wood, and got a heat gun, and melted them, and covered the hole that a horse kicked in my kick board.

It reminded me of the process that the work with horses like this is: because there has been some pretty fucked up stuff that has happened to them, enough to make them feel like they have to hurt their bodies to protect themselves from our hands. That painting is what healing looks like. Sometimes we have emotional scar tissue that keloids. But the thing is, the fact that we spend the time to try and create something that's beautiful, instead of throwing the piece of wood away and replacing it with a newly painted piece of wood… It brings life to the space and is proof of a life lived.

My work with him is like that. He's like, "AHHHHHHHH, YOU'RE QUESTION IS SUPPOSED TO HURT."
  "What if you breathe into it?"
  "I'M AFRAID TO BREATHE INTO IT."
  "Why are you afraid to breathe into it?"
  "BREATHING INTO IT REQUIRES BEING VULNERABLE."
  "What's so scary about being vulnerable?"
  "IF I DON'T PROTECT MYSELF, I'm afraid of having my body taken away from me without my permission."

35)

That's this whole conversation.

And I'll say, "Ok, where does it start?

He said, "It starts with me hearing you think about what you want to ask me."

I'm like, "Ok, great."

And he goes, "You know what, Nahshon, what has happened is that I can hear what you're thinking about asking me.

I go, "Okay, we're gonna think about trotting."

He goes, "Oh, that's kind of scary."

And so we stay there and work with him in that space.

So I say, "What happens to make you feel afraid of me thinking about trotting?"

He goes, "Well, when you think about trotting, I felt you not breathe all the way down into your belly. You were only breathing in your chest."

36]

Look at her on the other side of the arena. Look at how far away from you she is; and how the closer you get, the more agitated she becomes. That's a lot. And it goes to show you how those florets of fear that are blooming in her heart got planted there.

Then it's not like you don't have the skills for this. But rather, are you prepared to go that deep? Are you prepared to go journeying into the exploration of that question? Because if you decide to do it, there are going to be parts of yourself that need to be healed enough to help heal her. Or, are you healed enough to know that you can't help her?

Look at what that admission that it might not be what we want it to be has done. It's made her feel safe to walk across the arena because now she feels safe enough to not stay so far away. That's what softness is with this mare: it's sitting with those broken pieces of yourself and saying, I'm not perfect, and I need you to help put this question into an answer. That's what healing work is. And that's what someone who knows how to heal does. They know that the wisdom is in the lessons we're learning now.

36)

Your horse's heart-hurt is not hers. It's the person who gave it to her. And the question then becomes: do you, as someone who's supposed to help this mare, have the grace to have compassion for the people who did this to her? I can tell you, it's painful work. It's painful…it's painful work. Because you begin to see your hurts inside of theirs, and then you have to forgive the people who gave those memories to you. That's the only way forward.

It saddens me that a lot of horses are treated the way they are. It saddens me, too, that I've had to grow out of some of the stuff I've had to grow out of to learn how to truly connect with horses in the amplified energy and synchronicity of crystal clear consciousness, which is really just the horse's connection to consciousness reflecting back to me in those places within myself that consciousness has not yet reached.

Sometimes, I'm in total alignment, like the earth the sun, and the super flower blood moon during a lunar eclipse. Other times, I get lost in thought on things like how hard it is to, sometimes, just accept the question.

37]

1)

"I feel like I'm so stuck in my body that my molly can't hear me."

"What does that mean?"

"I can't find words to answer your question."

"Describe it to me as if it were a picture."

"There's a rope wrapped tightly around my waist on one end. It's attached to a tree on the other. It won't let me get too far when I try to walk away."

"What is the rope?"

"Judgement…shame… expectation….self-doubt…not being good enough… That kinda shit, ya' know: 'You gotta be perfect. You gotta get all of it done. You can't make a mistake."

"What is the tree?"

"All of the people who I feel that way around. The takers."

"Huh!"

"My life is good, though. I just want to be better for my mule."

2)

Ok. So, I want you to conjure up the thought, or the place, or the person with whom you feel the most safe, and let that be

37)

the only thought you hold. And I want you to warm it up as if you were able to with a thermostat. Warm it up more. And then let the safety-warmth blossom out of your pores. Be worthy of that. And questions about you deserving of feeling safe come up, I know. Breathe into those questions and offer them safety too. That's it.

Now, let the warmth allow your muscles to start to relax. Let it loosen them up. Loose enough for you to take a breath, you can feel all the way in your feet. Good, now at the base of your neck, warm it up. Warm, warm, warm, and breathe… breathe into it. There. Very good.

You're having trouble. Here, take these stones. Hold the purple one. Give it all to the stone. Let whatever comes, come. Breathe it into the stone, that Holy Child. My crystals are my Holy Children, like Maria Sabina's mushrooms. Forgive it. Yeah, very good. Breathe into those spaces where emotion has locked your body up so that you can move again. Trust it.

The tension on the left side of your neck, breathe into it. Yeah, spread your toes out so you can open the center of your feet and ground. That's it. Just breathe where there's room. Breathe into the spaces you have the courage to. Very good. And whatever thoughts are coming up when you breathe into those spaces, whose-ever showing up, try hard to forgive them.

And know, there's likely no apology on the horizon for the

deep-reaching breaches of trust that some of your past hearthurts are. But we grow by surrendering to growth. Worlds are created to be manipulated. That said, letting go is a journey full of unexpected surprises like the stages of grief. Grief can be lonely. Sometimes, grief is terrifying, and often times it hurts. Breathe into it.

Look! Who's there? Breathe into that. It's your body waking up. You're getting into a scary spot. Breathe into it... Breathe into it if you can. Breathe as courageously as you can into it. Trust your breath. Trust your breath before you trust yourself, and follow it. That's how you heal horses.

Good job. Very good. Breathe into it. Don't rush through it. Breathe into the stuck-point. Breathe into it. Create space with the breath. It seems impossible until you realize that raindrops fill the lake. Breathe into it, in-between the shoulders. Breathe.

And I think the thing waiting for you to realize it is that you must give yourself permission to heal, and you must give yourself permission to be free.

At the base of the neck, where the spinal cord meets the skull, there is an energy center. Breathe into that space. Very good. Make sure your tongue is to the roof of your mouth so that your face muscles relax...

And instead of finding a place where you're stuck and allow-

37)

ing trying to be the reason why we retreat, just stay there. Just stay there, and breathe into that spot. We're not going to retreat, recalibrate, and attack. We're just going to sit with it, like a yogi meditating on the corner of a busy intersection in New York City or the South Side of Chicago.

Whatever spaces are opening, allow the breath to move into that space. Very good. Trust it, I know it's hard for you to trust much… Very Good. Very good. Breathe into it. Breathe into it. Breathe into it. Breathe into everything. That's the lesson. That's it. Breathe into it. Breathe into it, and let it know that it's okay. And understanding, too, that the anxiety is worthy of love. And that the only reason it's so strong is that we try to push it away. Embrace it.

Good. You might be sore tonight. But look at how quiet and relaxed your mule is. I think that's enough.

38]

1)
This afternoon, I was having lunch with my nieces. When I asked what they thought about the title of this book, the oldest, who's five, began speaking in poetry and said:

"Legend has it; if you find the treasure, then you can…"
Where will the treasure be?
"Under the ocean, in a cave."

If you find the treasure under the ocean, in a cave…..
"…A golden mane will appear up, and then a golden horse, and then the person will appear."

So, if you find the treasure, under the sea, in a cave, then a golden mane will appear, and the horse and rider will what?
"…Will reappear, and they will come to life, again."

2)
The next day I called my oldest niece and told her, "This is what was said yesterday at lunch would sound like as a poem:"

38)

Legend has it

That if you find the treasure under the ocean in a cave

A golden mane will re-appear

And the horse and rider will live again

3)

"Yes," She said, "awesome."

Beautiful, I said.

She said, "Yeah, that's a good poem."

"What do you want to call it," I asked.

She said, "I haven't thought about what I want to call it yet. Can you give me another day to think about it, and I'll call you tomorrow?"

39]

If I can't love those challenging parts of who I am, how can I love a horse who's reflecting my challenging parts back to me like a mirror? For me, this is the heart of connection creation between horses and humans: where I'm no longer afraid of not being happy and it has changed my world. In that place of joy, I've learned how to celebrate what needs to be celebrated, which is the try, which is the acceptance of enough and growing that into an answer. It's a beautiful space, and my horses are changing for the better because of it.

And that's the reason I love my horses: each with all of their own baggage, because they let me know where I am now and where I'm not anymore, like people who bring who they need to hold them back so that they can't move forward. I just don't live in that space anymore, where what happens is what often happens when what is known and needs to be spoken isn't spoken, and you become a casket for someone else's secrets.

And then there were all of the ghosts that you brought to our lessons, and you were able to see the value that they had or didn't have, and you had the courage to try the situation without them, and you found a different part of yourself in that place. And though I haven't known you for much of that undoing, I do know that your horse's body was space that a lot of your ghosts felt safe inside of, and so working with you, through him, with that space, is the magic of horses for me.

A while ago, I had a horse who came to work with me in a clinic, whose person, at the beginning of their lesson, explained how the horse had bucked her off really bad and how she'd sent the horse to a trainer to get the horse to canter. The trainer used spurs and whips just to get the horse to go, and it just made the horse more angry. After which she asked what I thought about the horse and where they should start.

And then she shared how the horse had its stifles injected, and as a side note, that she named this horse after her father. As soon as she said that, the horse raised his head and neck, and his back visibly became tight. I asked if the vet had looked at the gelding's lumbar spine. She said they hadn't. I told her it might not be a bad thing to consider. She said "OK" and then proceeded to do groundwork with him.

And so she goes and starts trying to do this groundwork with this horse, and he totally, totally, totally is just not engaged. The whole time, while she's taking him to do this or that, he's braced in his neck, and she's breathing high up in her chest. So, I asked the lady if I could try, and after she handed me the rope and the horse turned around, walked up to me, and put his forehead right in my solar plexus. I looked at his person, and I looked at their trainer, who I asked if she'd seen what had just happened. The trainer nodded her head yes. Then I asked the lady to come back and take up the rope again, which she did. The horse went right back into hiding behind her tension.

So, we start talking some more, and I ask her to breathe into her body, and then my back just gets horribly tight and starts to ache. I asked if she felt any tightness in her lower back, and she said, "Yes." I asked her if she could please breathe into that tightness. As she did, she began to weep. Then I asked her the reason she named her horse after her father.

Between questions, I had her take walk breaks. As she answered me, the horse became more and more relaxed: letting his head down, licking-and chewing, taking deep, full-body breaths, and his lower lip got floppy. And as they walked around the arena, his hips opened up, and his barrel is just swinging, swinging, swinging…

And then she comes back after having used the walk about to try and get herself together, and when she does, he starts breathing in her chest again, and the horse's lower back starts to tighten again, and I tell her, "Okay, breathe deeper. Deep down into your belly. When we breathe in our chest, that's where we are living in belief, and it's like falling in love, which is easy to do. It makes you blind." I said, "Breathe in your belly, that place of knowingness…"

She went on to share how her father passed away when she was a young woman. As she continues on, with some of the circumstances around which she wasn't able to say goodbye, the horse drops his neck, starts to yawn, and starts to pass gas, and his whole back lifts up.

"Your dad, he still comes and visits you, doesn't he?"
She agreed.
"And sometimes you feel him trying to talk to you and tell you something, don't you?"
She agreed, again and again when I'd said how I felt him just show up here, with us.
And I said, "What did he just tell you?
"That everything's okay," She said.

After which, her horse gently bit her on the ass. That was the end of the lesson.

Before they left the arena, she said, "I got a therapy session, but came for a horsemanship lesson." I told her, "I'm a horseman. I'm not a therapist." I continued, "I think the difference between the two is that the purpose of a therapist is to help people heal their past to get there—to the future. My work is to help people heal the past to get here—to the present. The present is where horse-humanship starts.

40]

I also can't say that if you take a horse like him, and all of mine, who've been the landfill for someone else's past life secrets, that the process of helping them heal isn't going to be easy, or fast, or what you think they should be able to do.

When you deal with a horse who has obviously had some really tough situations in his life, you have to understand that sometimes offering them a better life doesn't make any horrible memories from their past go away.

I have a mare, who I've had for, going on, four years. My mare Mohawk. And, I've had a lot of success with almost every horse I've ever touched, and this mare, no matter how helpful I am for other people and their horses, there are just some things that I really have trouble understanding about her.

I do know that she's my horse. I don't necessarily know why she's mine. And, I did kind of like you, after about six months, just started riding her again because there's so much that I didn't understand.

I still leave room and possibility for her to get further than we are because I think that that's a really important way to live life: for the possibility to always have room to exist. But, she…she likely won't reach the level of my other horses. But I don't know.

So, I think the thing that's really important for me, right now, is that you understand the reason that you have him, and the reason that you ride, and prepare yourself for his best to be enough…, even if it's not everything that you want. It can also be more than you expected, though. I can't make any promises on either end because it's his choice.

I say that because you're young, and it's important that I be very honest with you, that one of the hardest lessons that horses make you accept if you have any heart at all, is what enough, for now, means and looks like.

I think why I'm feeling like I have to over-explain this is because I've seen so many good horses given up on. I asked you those questions because if you're not clear about the process of bringing a horse to that place, trust, then you don't have a point of reference for him to answer based on his individual stage of development.

I think that, as a teacher, it's my job to tell you this: he can't give you the right answer if you're asking the wrong question. But, I think that it is really important for you, especially with you being a young rider of such magnitude and possibility, to really grow in the way of seeing when your horse isn't answering the question in that way that I would want him to, to ask yourself, "Am I asking the horse in the way that she or he is able to understand?" When horses don't answer my questions, I always look at myself as the problem first.

I will say this, there are many things about this horse's conformation that aren't ideal, but he is willing to try. Which means that, as long as you have him, you have to be willing to accept the pieces of try as the correct answer until he's able to build the whole answer to completion. Do you hear what I'm saying to you?

You're at this point where you have a horse that is requiring the work with him to be more than just fun, like riding a jet ski, or a snow mobile, or a mountain bike. He's turning you into a human being by teaching you about compassion, and acceptance, and the lessons life teaches you with the choices you make.

These are hard lessons, sometimes.

41]

Only ask questions that are answerable. Right now, nothing is answerable but this: He's working through his emotions so that he can find feeling. And emotions are like raccoons holding on to something shiny all night long: they don't let go.

And so this is just convincing the raccoon to let go of the shiny thing, and you can see the breath starting to go down deeper in his body, now the tempo of the walk is starting to slow down, his neck is starting to lower: he's processing his feelings. He has a right to feel how he feels. That doesn't mean that world stops. There are no slaves, horse nor human.

And I think that that's the important thing to see: people aren't as far away from horses as people believe. When horses are too far away, they turn into an alien planet whose language we do not know. Then the relationship becomes abusive because "no" doesn't exist: It creates people who bully people, people who bully horses, and horses who bully people. "No" is very important. It's like the golden thread. If "no" is not an option, then "yes" is not true.

And that's the thing: this horse only allows himself to be

ridden when he knows that "no" would be respected. Every other time he just shut his back down. I mean, sometimes walking like his front legs have been sawed off at the knee. Just because he didn't know if "no" would be honored. Even voicing this is calming him down.

I think it is incredibly important that all horses, and people too, learn how to self-regulate. That means that people have to stop allowing the art of being afraid to be so valuable that we can't find softness enough to just let the agitated horse find itself in peace, safely, of course: A horse that is spooked and runs off will stop sooner if you go with it instead of trying to stop it. But, do you trust yourself to stay in that soft space?

And that's it, I think: when we are the center of the system, we try and make the horse look to us for answers. When we are a part of the system, the horse and the person look to each other, and everything comes out of each other. Because it's a lie to say that I know everything that he needs at this moment. I know that I can listen. I know that I can keep myself still by following him and give him the opportunity to process.

It's taken him ten minutes to bring himself down. This is the longest he's stood still today so far. And it's understanding that until we get to this point no work can happen. There's nothing available. This whole process with me in this part of you and your horse's realm has been to get him to trust that

I don't have an agenda other than giving him what he needs.

The only personal attachment to an outcome for him is him finding calm and quiet. Out of that, he's found the courage to try and answer every question that I've asked because he knows that I'm not going to ask him an unanswerable question. It may take me three weeks to teach him how to build the correct answer, but it comes: as long as the lesson is relaxed and our questions are healthy.

Now we're getting a nice walk that I can begin to ask for something out of. So, I'll ask for him to soften and lift the shoulder and still not change the rhythm of the walk. And I'll ask for him to bend and start lifting his back up. What I'm trying to say is that the lesson must grow out of where the horse is at, not where we want the horse to be. It shouldn't be a whole page turned. It should be the next word. That's the only way to really write a story: the next word.

This is how we build "yes-es" out of "no-s." We respect it. That's trust. I think that value in that for horses lay in them knowing that you understand that when you don't try to take what you want from them, they offer more than you knew they were capable of. They offer you so much more. I think that's the magic of horses, I think, especially if they're coming out of the memory of a hurt-filled situation from which they've chosen to give us another chance: in the beginning, they kill time to reveal our hearts. The secret to healing horses is waiting. It allows broken horses the space to learn how to believe in themselves. Confidence in a person's hands is what makes a horse beautiful under saddle.

And you realize that the people that hurt him, training-wise, that's the best they had to offer, that's where they are on their journey. If our journey is true, we've been there, too. Does that make the hurt right, or excuse it? No. But it is what it is: you can only give what you have. I think that's the wonderful invitation that horses offer: the opportunity to become more beautiful. That's where miracles live: in letting go enough to grow...

42]

I think, if anything, your horse is a journey back to your own voice. I have a mala that's made out of one hundred and eight yak bone skull-shaped beads that I use to meditate on impermanence while I recite this chant, *I live to die. I love people to lose them. I have horses to let them go*, over and over again, until *Amen*.

I often think about how being human means life is a game that must be played with choices like chess pieces and how horses have acres of answers to our questions when they are allowed to speak, and we listen: every horse I've ever met is the best horse I've ever known.

I just want you to be available to your horse's breath enough to follow it with your breath. Close your eyes. I want you to feel your horse breathing with your body. It's OK. Just breathe. Find his breath.

Good. Now, open your eyes and try to match your breath to his. Then you'll feel him start to relax because he knows you hear him. You see how the anxiety's starting to lessen. Do you feel your muscles loosening a little bit? Yeah, that's him taking the temperature down.

You feel how his back is coming up, and he's beginning to hold you like a buoy in the ocean? Good, now feel his hind legs in your seat bones. The correct rider's position is a soft-touch-filled invitation for the horse to relax inside our voice. Every time a seat bone goes up, that's his hind leg under your body.

And let your belly relax, and you'll start feeling his hind legs in your rib cage, and you'll start moving from side to side, just like if you were walking. Like that.

Think about sending the breath down to your belly button. Push your belly out with the breath, and it'll open up your back. The more the breath opens the belly, the softer the butt cheeks become, and the more your spine is available to his movement...your lower back. Good.

Did you feel him slow down? Good. Yeah, you're getting there. Perfect. Perfect. Release your lower back. That's where all of the doubt hides: your stomach being pulled in, your chest opens, and your back straight... Posturing. Release all that shit, and just breathe into it, don't force it.

You want to be polite with your breath. Like a raindrop down a window pane, it makes its way because it just flows into the space that's already there. Don't try to create space. Go where there's an opening.

At first, it's going to be small, like the silence between the notes of a Meadowlark's song. Don't try and make that silence last longer than it lasts. People try to make emptiness too deep. It's not super-deep. That space between the inhale and the exhale is the sound of one hand clapping.

Now we're gonna create some space in your spine, and what I want you to do is close your lips and let the tips of your bottom and top teeth touch. Now put the top of your tongue to the roof of your mouth, and press up with your tongue. It'll bring your chin in and create length in your whole spine.

You feel his back coming up a little bit? Yeah? Good. Good. That's all you. Just follow the movement. The more you follow, the more you relax, but you're gonna have all these things, with their reasons, showing up in your head who are gonna tell you that should be tense and why. Just let them pass like time. Shit's coming up. Let it go. And let him open up your spine.

Good. That trouble that you're feeling in the muscles, if you breathe into them, those things that are wanting to fight leaving you so that they can go on and fulfill their destiny, you feel them? That is what he came in here doing today. That's all the memories living in the muscles that you didn't know were there. Crazy, huh?

The past hides in the body, not the mind. And so, if you keep breathing into those spaces that are opening up, he'll start to relax. Keep focusing on that space. See, he's starting to slow down. He runs from people running from their ghosts. And if you just lean into it... lean into it... Yes. Very good.

When I was in Nepal, they had these old old temples there, in Durbar Square, that had all of these really, what was supposed to be, scary faced images carved out of wood on the outside of the temple. As I understand it, they were meant to ward off anyone who was not a true seeker of inner peace, like those thoughts that are blossoming out of your body, and how once you moved beyond them, then you were inside, and it was the most peaceful feeling...

When you move beyond that space of thought, there's just love, emptiness. And that's the space that you have to allow yourself to be worthy of and be nourished in. And you see when you let him move your body, how balanced you are. Wherever you are at, follow that...follow that...

Good, and what you might start feeling is some tightness around your throat. That tightness is your ghosts trying to keep you away from your voice. Breathe into that space. Breathe into it, don't push it away. Good. Breathe into it. Good. Stay there. Lean into it. Good. Perfect. That's it, don't push it away. It's hard. Lean into it. You're finding it. Very good. Good. Good. Good. Told you, your horse is a bridge. He lives in the space between here and there, where the cause and effect are the same things.

When you move beyond those skillfully whittled scary imag-

42)

inings carved on the front of the temple, you find the clarity of a full moon in a cloudless blue morning sky: your mind is quiet and free from distraction like a snowflake dissolving in thin air; or the still, inward silence that's found in the sound of one hand clapping; and your horse stops running from you running from your ghosts… your past.

The simplicity of all may not make logical sense to you, which is not easy, I know. But, when we allow ourselves to not be addicted to logic, we begin to realize all of our potential. You just allowed yourself to claim that freedom. Good job. Good job. You feel how much space there is? I told you I'd teach you how to ride a horse. This is the first lesson: take no thought.

43]

Just let him move. It's okay. I think the important part in this is making sure that you stay breathing in your belly, and the reason is… and a horse taught me this last I was here when he came and put his forehead into my abdomen, I went home and did some research; belly breathing is how we access the parasympathetic nervous system.

If we breathe in our chest, as I understand it, we're in survival mode at the center of the circle, trying not to drown in our emotions. When we let our mind go down into our belly, we're able to stop let go enough to heal, and see, and listen, and observe, and float in feel. So, let's start there. Let the breath move your belly.

Good. Now, bring your mind a little lower in your body, maybe your thighs. Yeah! Then walk, and we'll do it again. This is why I love thoroughbreds because we think they're clairvoyant, but they just really listen, and they trust you with what you say. So, to get him to stop, we'll use the mind. Bring your mind down to your thighs, again. And then, take it back up to your belly and walk.

See, I struggle with that same anxiety because, you know, it's like, "Just stop your horse with your mind." You know, and they probably are like, "This guy is a kook." But it works. I understand where you're coming from, so we're just going to be courageous together.

Let's go in the other direction. Now, halt. Just bring the mind down to the thigh and just wait for him to hear you. Yes, very good. And walk. This is the magic of Thoroughbreds. I love them so much. They can be quite difficult: I have a mare that makes me feel like a total idiot most of the time, but when I understand what she's trying to tell and say it correctly, she does what I ask right away. My geldings are more merciful than my mares. I'm convinced that the reason more Thoroughbreds don't make it is that we just aid them too much.

And about his challenges around contact: I don't know if you're a nerd like me, but I like to just look up at the sky and watch birds fly. And, I understood the use of the chest as an aid by watching birds fly like earth angels sending us messages through movement, like a beautiful dancer. Look! Turkey Vultures.

And you see that when their wings are up, their hearts are open. That's how we raise the horse's neck and bring them into a more vertical balance, by mimicking a bird in flapping flight. If you keep breathing in your belly, then drop your reins and put your hands on your hips, that's the feeling. Now, if you extend your arms straight out in front of you, you'll be mimicking a bird in bounding flight, and that will lower the horse's neck and put it into a more horizontal balance. This is a way that, maybe, we can help him feel a bit safer putting his hind legs into our hands and coming into contact with the rein.

So, when you're ready, let's give it a try. And what I'd like you to try, is when you open your heart, keep your elbow gently bent, and it will naturally bring the hand up. And bounding flight, and we'll come to a lengthening. Yes, again, thumbs up, so you're not putting unnecessary pressure on his poll. Flapping flight. Bounding flight, lengthen. And so now he starts to find the hand because his neck is following your chest. Very good. That's how we can bring a horse into contact with the hand.

Now, opening the heart and putting your shoulders back isn't the same thing. The latter stiffens your back, and then your seat can't move. We need the lower back to stay supple because that's where we first integrate the movement from the horse's hind legs into our bodies.

Let's try it again, and what I want you to think about, and I hope it will help with your hip, is keeping your ankles in line with your neck and your head over your pelvis instead of the ear-shoulder-hip-heel line. You'll feel your hip flexors open up without the strain. Do you feel how his walk just improved? Now, open the heart. Let the hands follow the chest… When you open, let the arms bend. Keep them at a ninety-degree angle, and then they'll lift. Now, soften your chest and ask him to lower his neck. Very good. Just let him find you. Let him find you. Keep walking in your thighs. Neck control without pulling is so important.

What I want you to do now, is with your belly relaxed out, think about pulling your belt buckle up to your belly button and will lengthen your back without making it tense, and it will ask him to start tipping his pelvis forward and lowering his sacrum. Yeah yeah yeah. Release it. This is the beginning of collection.

Now, don't lean back: keep your ankles in line with your neck. There, now open your heart. There's his back lifting him into a beautiful trot transition. That's how you create impulsion without pressure. That was beautiful.

Also, I think you need to give yourself more credit. I really do. You make it sound like you're a shit rider, and you're not. Look at what you just did: you just brought this horse into collection without taking anything away from him. And I think there's a difference between incompetence and ignorance. A big one. And I think that if you come in thinking that you know everything there is to know, you might as well be dead because you're no real good. You're not helpful because you won't grow.

This is the practice of meeting horses where they're at and working from there. You can't listen if they can't talk, and then things start going terribly wrong. This lesson today was you getting a surrogate for the response that your hands would get without needing them: the chest. Good work. Good work, indeed.

44]

A few weeks ago, I went and audited the clinic of two horsemen whose work I've studied since I was kiddo, and I got to meet them and that was also great. I went to try and find help for my mare, Mohawk, and I didn't find it. Not to say that it wasn't there, maybe it just wasn't time. But, my mare is coming along.

It's the strangest thing when you can help other people and their horses in the ways that you wish yours would. And sometimes, the best answer you have, regardless of all that you know is "I don't know," and you look for help and there is none.

She's done an incredible turn around: she's feeling a lot better in her body. She's able to stand on the SureFoot Pads. Last year they made her explode... too much sensory input. She was super dis-regulated. But, her nervous system is recalibrating, she's learning how to self-regulate... Her pelvis is lifted, the lumbar bump from her pelvic fracture is flattening out, and her hunter's bump is getting smaller.

I've waited for Mohawk to stop being disinterested about being broken for so long that she thought she couldn't be fixed. But, love has changed how she thinks about her body. I think the main reason I'm sharing this story with you is to tell you how over-and-over again I've learned that when you're not afraid to take the time, you have more than you need like an old Sequoia tree. But, if you're in a rush, like a hummingbird, you never have enough time.

And how, regardless of all of the information that we have: all of the books, and all of the people with their beautiful minds who are helping guide our way through our journey with our horses, the answer to each horse is each horse, just like the answer to each person is each person. And I've been thinking: What is a horse but and person's teachers? And what is what is a person but a horse's job? I'm thankful that my horses keep working on me like an embodiment of the light.

My work has morphed into a meditation on how balance is movement, and how movement is life, and how life is a balance between carrying and being carried, which is the journey of power, and wholeness, and healing, and the holy in every step. The deeper I go into this work with horses the more this work with horses become my spiritual home. How we see determines how we hear... if I look at the horse and only see the horse for me, I don't hear what the horse really has to say... If I look at the horse and see the horse for the horse, then the horse knows that I'm listening. What I've learned about horses is that when we listen to them they take that as an act of love for them on our part... And the magic about horses is that when they know you love them, they offer you their power in return, and they teach you, they teach you how to use it because they trust you.

You work with the horse you have today, and not with the horse you want tomorrow. You have to do that with you too: you work with the you you are, and not the you you want to be. When you train a horse like their life depends on it, you go slow. That said, it's working with horses as individuals that grows a human being.

That's the beauty of horses in the human heart, they can make it bloom like a lotus blossoming in the warmth of early morning light beams, into a beautiful thing, out of shit and mud and stink. All of the possibilities blooming out of all the life we've lived; and how we can still offer something useful… from the shit, like a garden. That's what horses are for me, and that's what they're teaching me to be for people. They can heal every human hurt. They can't cure life, but they can heal it.

It's a process of becoming as clear as possible about the reason horses are in your life, and it's different for every person. Mine is to learn how to try and help horses be happier in human lives. It's learning how to take a broken thing that nobody else thinks is possible and asking what they need from me to still be alive, if they want to. Healthy relationships are physical and emotionally safe places of consent where the less attached you become, the more connected you become. It's like realizing that we start off like a handful of arena sand clouding our communication with horses, and as they open us up our voice becomes more and more clear. There's no more sand left to slip through our fingers because we're not afraid of letting go of all the shit that is not us.

If there's so much confusion about what should happen, it's because there's an abundance of a lack of clarity. You don't get more clear by continuing to practice not being clear. You have to learn first that you're not being clear. You have to see that. I see that in horses continuing to be what is not helpful for mutual consideration, and how their horses are balancing that behavior in something that I'm presenting to them. So, if I want a troubled horse to be possible, I have to change.

I have to change if I want you to feel safe enough to take this whole hour to talk about you learning to work through you lack of clarity, I have to make myself available to you for you to feel safe enough to say "this is what I need…" to really trust that I don't expect you to perform for me: I'm my students devoted and helpful follower so that my students can hopefully be devoted and helpful followers of the horse.

At the heart of it all, for me, is continuing to try and help people trust themselves, again: instead of thinking I expect you to do something that doesn't feel healthy to you, tell me. I'll try and find another way. If I can't I'll try and help you find someone else who can.

Miracles happen outside of our comfort zone, things are

possible when we don't have to be responsible for everything being possible. The magic is life itself. This is the process of the answer we need to offer horses: Horses need to feel like we're safe enough for us to be a safe space for them, then they relax. You're mare didn't change one bit, you did. Every change that occurred, we made, and she felt safer and safer and safer inside of the space that was offered, that's horse-humanship.

45]

Dear future self,

I've been asked to write a letter for you to read the next time you're thirteen years old and are beginning to see glimpses of what your life with horses will be. The most important thing I can tell you is stay weird—it'll teach you to trust your heart, and your heart will teach you to trust life. When you trust life, you're not afraid to change. Not being afraid to change is what will teach you how to be a human being. Human beings help.

Help is what you were and are and will be, always—for those who want it. Some will, some won't. That's life. Try to shoot for a breakthrough every morning, as there's no use in your fighting the growth into who you are.

Also, know that people will make fun of you out of a need to stay blind to those not-so-understood places in themselves that they're too afraid of to see. This time is because you're Black, or gay, or too Black, or a male, or not Black enough, or free, or whatever else they can find to try and make you feel like you're too far away to be worthy of their love. Next time it'll be something else. Be kind to yourself, always, and stay as

45)

kind as you can to others when they press your boundaries.

That said, have boundaries, I once heard a boundary defined like this: "I have to have you right here, not there, so that we can be now, and not then, again," without guilt, or shame. Boundaries will help you be more brave than you feel. Boundaries will help you know that you need to leave when you want to stay, or that you need to stay when you want to leave. Boundaries are love. Love the ones who love you back and leave the rest alone. And keep following your horses, they'll teach you to find heaven in every step. Love is big, the world is small. Be love.

Again, know that people will point. Sometimes, you won't understand the reason until later. Sometimes, you won't understand at all. Either way, learn to stay intelligent. And know this, intelligence isn't belief in what is true, but rather a process by which you take organic truth and work with it enough to step into the next step from the untold years, and possibilities, and relationships that are hidden therein. So, keep studying the old answers, and keep exploring new ideas, and meditate, and practice being intentional enough with your dreams to write them down so that you stay free: this is prayer. And when you find this, look me up. It'll help you remember.

Your past self,
Nahshon Cook

P.S:

A life following horses is a life of true peace. On the outside, it looks really boring. But on the inside, it can heal the earth, it can heal every human heart hurt. And it's all built around accepting the gift that horses give humans to not be greedy.

Ninety percent of what happens in my arena is not in any book I read. But rather, what shows up at the door. The heart of my work is safety. The work is safe. This way of working is not evangelical because it's too small, like an ant: Safety. Make yourself safe enough to be safe, that's all horse want from us. And there's so much shit that we work through to get there: our parents, or the world, our prejudices, and other people's prejudices, and all of these things that are supposed to matter that really don't matter.

And people come to the place where you are, and people have all of this shit on the floor, in front of them, that they've unpacked from inside of themselves, and they can walk away, and let it go, and be brand new, and start over. No matter where I am, I can let all this shit go and start over. I don't have to carry this anymore. That's the gift of horses asking us if we have the courage to be here right now forever. Almost all of the horses I work with are only possible outside of the confines of what other people think they deserve.

Take Mohawk for example, how do I know she's getting better? She's not trying to kill me anymore. She had to feel safe enough to stop trying to kill me. She learned how well threatening people worked until it didn't work anymore. In that mare, I saw every bully that I'd ever had in my whole life so far, and she was my door for me to make peace with them trying to hurt me for my love of my horses teaching me to love myself. She's helped my gifts get stronger. My agreement with life is to be helpful.

So much of this work, again, is found in horses like Mohawk and Jericho who give you the gift of not allowing yourself to be greedy, and how much you get in return, because you can't just take what you want. You have to be satisfied with what they offer, and then they just begin to bloom like a lotus flower in the early morning sun. The path of horses in people's lives is very different than the path of people in horse's lives. They are very different worlds. For my work to be helpful for some people, they have to change how they see their horses. That's really hard for a lot of people. Some people can't do it. But I can, I'm thankful for that.

That said, there are some things that work out, like this whole life that I'm living, that do not make sense. There are mornings that, after I wake up, I have to remind myself that this is happening today. That said, if it's ever warranted, write me a letter, and if I don't write back for some reason, know that the only thing I'll ever tell you to do is trust yourself, just like you're learning to trust yourself on that horse, and how things change when you know where you are when you're there. It's always the same answer.

My step-dad told me something that changed my life, before he died. It was the last time we had dinner, and I hear his voice every time I'm stuck. He said, "Nahshon, you first. You first, fuck everybody else." You know what, you cant help nobody if you don't help you. What does you first look like? And know, that there will come a day when you outgrown the lifetimes of information you've amassed, and you'll have the have to make the choice to continue doing what we've outgrown so we don't have to change, or have the courage to begin again.

I feel like I'm starting to ramble, so I'll start winding this down. From the very beginning, mine has been a commitment to love, and to embody that as much as I could. And I think that what I've been trying to say this whole letter long is that if you follow it, and your gift grows, you'll have to grow too. That's what being a horseman has taught me. That's the gift horses brought to my life: just keep walking until you can't walk no more. Then, rest… until you can start walking again. That's the story of every horse in my barn. And in that rest you get to know yourself, the story of the hurt, and if it's valuable to keep telling. It's a magical life…it's hard as hell, but anything worthwhile is. We lose our power to obstacles we give our power to: If they don't support you in your power, don't keep them close. If they matter, they'll change. And what a gift, because change is what makes life possible.

If you listen to your heart, your path will be made clear. But, if you're used to seeing the whole way where you're going,

45)

that's not going to happen. The clouds, I call them the cloud people, sometimes they come down, and its's so foggy because they just come down on to the land. And it's really just like they descend a flight of stairs and are walking around in the field. And they're taller than the house. And that's what this my path is like: it's so foggy that you can only see the next step. And then it clears and there you are. And it stays clear for a little bit, and then it's time to grow, and then the cloud people descend down the stairs from the sky again, and you keep walking. When you know how to not know, you know everything you need to know. Everything. You just need to take the next step.